Primary World Atlas

Globes and maps

Globes are models of the earth. The seven global views below show the true shape and size of the continents.

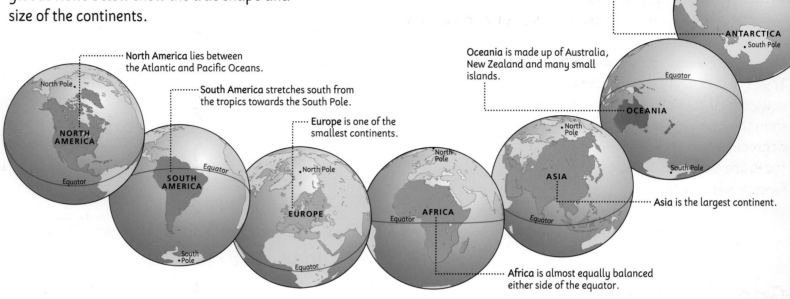

North America lies between the Atlantic and Pacific Oceans.

South America stretches south from the tropics towards the South Pole.

Europe is one of the smallest continents.

Antarctica encircles the South Pole.

Oceania is made up of Australia, New Zealand and many small islands.

Asia is the largest continent.

Africa is almost equally balanced either side of the equator.

Mapping the world

To show the world on a flat map we need to peel the surface of the globe and flatten it out. There are many different methods of altering the shape of the earth so that it can be mapped on an atlas page. These methods are called **projections**.

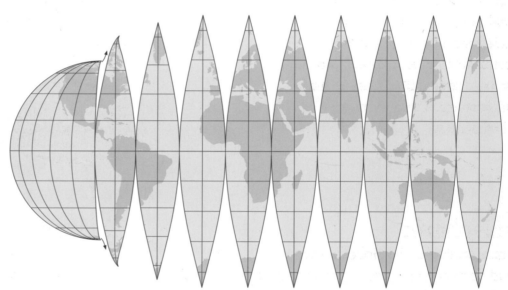

This is how the earth would look if the surface could be peeled and laid flat.

Projections

Map projections change the shape and size of the continents and oceans. The projection used for world maps in this atlas is called Eckert IV.

How the world map looks, depends on which continents are at the centre of the map. Compare the shape of Africa on the maps below to that on the globe.

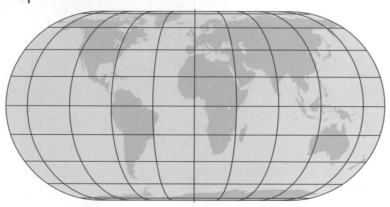

For UK atlases the world would look like this.

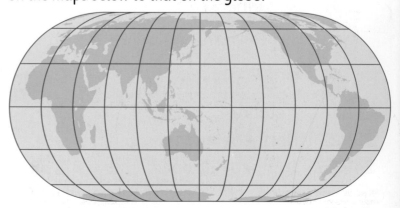

For Australian atlases the world would look like this.

Latitude and longitude

Every feature in the world can be located accurately. We use latitude and longitude to locate where features are. Latitude and longitude form our global positioning system.

Lines of latitude are imaginary lines which circle the earth. They are numbered in degrees North or South of the equator. Lines of longitude are imaginary lines which run from the North to the South Poles. They are numbered in degrees East or West of a line through London known as the Prime Meridian. We use the degrees to say where any feature is located.

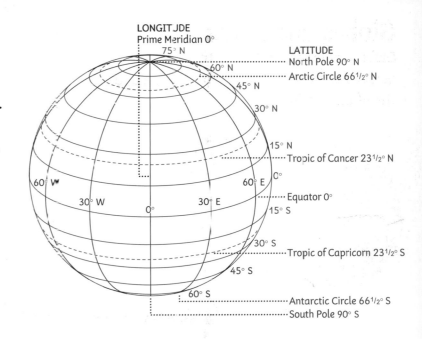

Grid references

Lines of latitude and longitude are used in this atlas to make a grid. By labelling the columns in the grid with a letter and the rows with a number a simple grid code e.g. B6 can be used to find all places within one grid square. This system is used in this atlas.

Cartagena is in B8

Bogotá is in B7

Piura is in A6

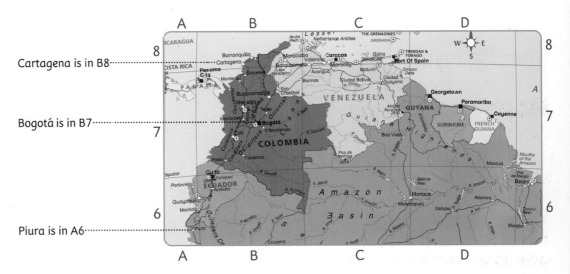

Hemispheres

The equator divides the globe into two imaginary halves. All land north of the equator is called the northern hemisphere. Land south of the equator is called the southern hemisphere. 0° and 180° lines of longitude also divide the globes into two imaginary halves, the western and eastern hemispheres.

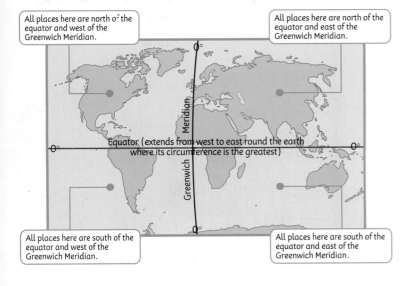

Direction

On most atlas maps you will find a compass. It names the four compass points North (N), East (E), South (S) and West (W). Between each main point are intermediate points Northeast, Southeast, Southwest and Northwest. These help us give more accurate directions.

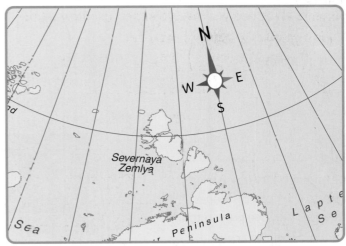

On atlas maps the north point always follows a line of longitude

Atlas maps

Atlas maps tell us about the various parts of the world. They tell us about different environments in the world.

Some maps show country shapes and where towns are located within the country. These are called political maps.

Some maps show landscapes. They show the physical environment.

Special names and numbers

Special names and numbers are used to label parts of an atlas map.

Title
This names the map area and describes what the map shows.

Page number
This helps you to find out where the map you want is in the atlas.

Locator map
This shows the part of the world covered by the map.

Area comparison
This map shows the size of the British Isles compared to the region mapped.

Scale
This explains how large a map is. It helps to work out distances between places. See page 6 to find out more about scale.

Compass
This always points north-south on the map. It shows east and west. Other directions can be found from the compass.

Key
This explains what the colours and symbols used on the map represent.

Fact boxes
These contain interesting information about a continent.

Map symbols

Maps are made up of symbols and names. The symbols can be points, lines or area colours.
A map is complete when the symbols and the names are combined.

Point symbols

- ■ Town stamps
- ▲ Mountain peaks
- ⊕ Airports

Lines

- —— Roads
- ⊢⊣⊢⊣ Railways
- —— Rivers and canals
- —— Coastline

Area colours

- ▭ Lake/sea
- ◿ Country colours

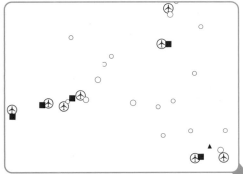

Point symbols are used on a map to show towns, mountain peaks and airports.

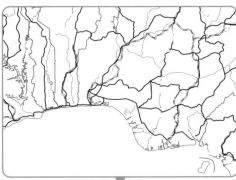

Lines are used an a map to show communications and drainage.

Area colours are used to distinguish one country from another and the land from the sea.

Names on atlas maps

The style and size of the type used on maps helps to explain what the name means.

Large bodies of water

PACIFIC OCEAN

Gulf of Guinea

Islands

Cuba

Bioco

Countries

N I G E R I A

BENIN

Large cities

Porto-Novo

Lomé

Small towns

Parakou

Enugu

Rivers

Mississippi

Nile

Amazon

Mountain peaks

Mount Cameroon

Everest

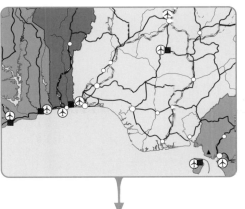

All the symbols are combined to show features and their correct locations.

Names are needed to show places and features shown on the map. Only some places and features are named.

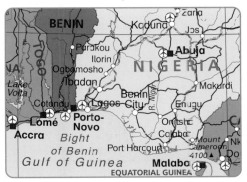

The map is complete when the symbols and the names are combined.

Scale

Maps are much smaller than the regions they show. To compare the real area with the mapped area you have to use a scale. Each map in this atlas shows its scale. This is shown using a scale bar which is explained in words.

E.g.
```
0    200    400    600    800 km
```

Scale : One centimetre on this map is the same as 200 kilometres on the ground.

Large scale maps show smaller areas with more detail.

LARGE SCALE

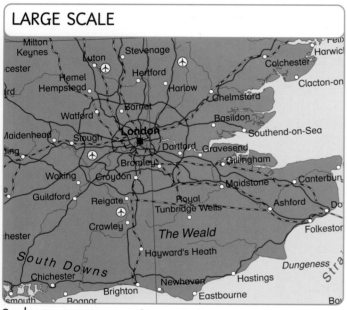

Scale: One centimetre on this map is the same as 20 kilometres on the ground.
```
0    20    40    60    80    100 km
```

MEDIUM SCALE

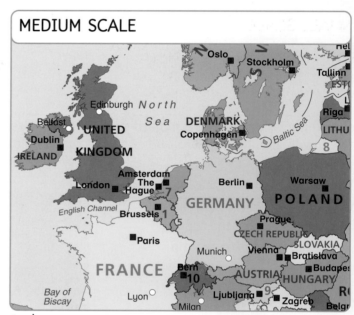

Scale: One centimetre on this map is the same as 250 kilometres on the ground.
```
0    250    500    750    1000    1250 km
```

Measuring distance

The scale of a map can be used to measure how far it is between two places. For example, the straight line distance between Boa Vista and Cayenne on the map to the right is 5 centimetres.

Look at the ruler.
One centimetre on this map is the same as 200 kilometres on the ground. The real distance between Boa Vista and Cayenne is therefore 1000 kilometres (i.e. 5 X 200).

```
0    200    400    600    800 km
```
Scale : One centimetre on this m[e]

Extend your knowledge and understanding by visiting these websites which provide lots of information and material to help with your homework and projects.

British Isles
Places to visit
Visit Britain www.visitbritain.com
Tourism in Ireland www.tourismireland.com
www.discoverireland.ie
Weather and climate
The Met Office www.metoffice.gov.uk
BBC weather www.bbc.co.uk/weather
Landscapes and rivers
Learning through landscapes www.ltl.org.uk
Learning rivers www.swgfl.org.uk/rivers
Scottish landscapes
www.bbc.co.uk/scotland/education/sysm/landscapes
Statistics
Nat onal statistics www.statistics.gov.uk/glance

Europe
European Union www.europa.eu.int/abc/index_en.htm

World
Climate
World climate statistics www.worldclimate.com
Population
City populations www.citypopulation.de
Geography
Royal Geographical Society www.rgs.org
National Geographic www.nationalgeographic.com
Mountains
Mountains of the world www.peakware.com
Satellite images
Earth Observatory earthobservatory.nasa.gov
Visible Earth visibleearth.nasa.gov
MODIS satellite images modis.gsfc.nasa.gov
Development issues
Global Eye www.globaleye.org.uk
Flags
Flags of the world www.theodora.com/flags
International organisations
ActionAid International www.actionaid.org
The Commonwealth www.youngcommonwealth.org
Christian Aid www.globalgang.org.uk
United Nations www.cyberschoolbus.un.org

Small scale maps show larger areas with less detail.

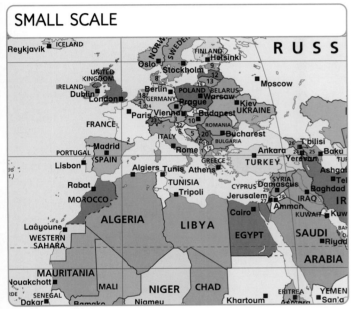

SMALL SCALE

Scale: One centimetre on this map is the same as 800 kilometres on the ground.

0   800   1600   2400   3200 km

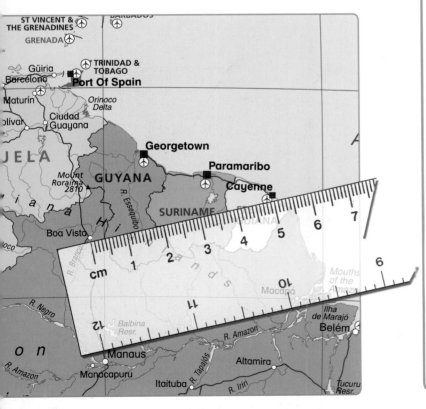

he same as 200 kilometres on the ground.

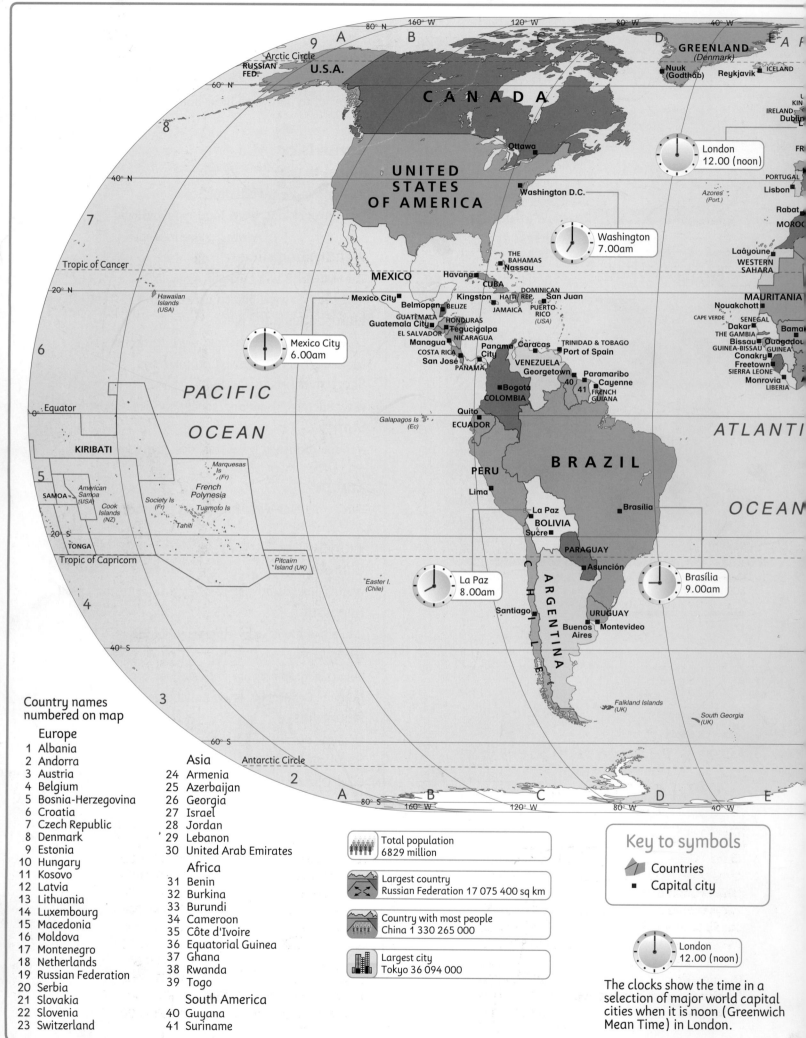

9 A B **C** **D** GREENLAND E
(Denmark)

Arctic Circle

RUSSIAN
FED.

U.S.A.

Nuuk
(Godthåb)

Reykjavik

ICELAND

C A N A D A

Ottawa

IRELAND

L
KIN

Dublin

London
12.00 (noon)

FR

UNITED
STATES
OF AMERICA

Washington D.C.

PORTUGAL

Azores
(Port.)

Lisbon

Washington
7.00am

Rabat

MOROC

Tropic of Cancer

THE
BAHAMAS

Nassau

Laâyoune

WESTERN
SAHARA

MEXICO

Havana

CUBA

DOMINICAN

MAURITANIA

Mexico City

Kingston

HAITI REP.

San Juan

Nouakchott

Belmopan

BELIZE

JAMAICA

PUERTO

CAPE VERDE

SENEGAL

Mexico City
6.00am

GUATEMALA

Guatemala City

HONDURAS

Tegucigalpa

RICO
(USA)

Dakar

THE GAMBIA

Bama

EL SALVADOR

NICARAGUA

Bissau

Ouagadou

Managua

Panama

Caracas

TRINIDAD & TOBAGO

GUINEA-BISSAU

GUINEA

COSTA RICA

City

Port of Spain

Conakry

San José

PANAMA

VENEZUELA

Freetown

Georgetown

Paramaribo

SIERRA LEONE

PACIFIC

Bogotá

40

Cayenne

Monrovia

COLOMBIA

41

FRENCH

LIBERIA

GUIANA

Quito

Hawaiian
Islands
(USA)

OCEAN

Galapagos Is
(Ec)

ECUADOR

ATLANTI

Equator

KIRIBATI

B R A Z I L

OCEAN

PERU

Marquesas
Is
(Fr)

Lima

SAMOA

American
Samoa
(USA)

French
Polynesia

La Paz

Brasília

Society Is
(Fr)

Cook
Islands
(NZ)

Tuamoto Is

BOLIVIA

Sucre

Tahiti

PARAGUAY

TONGA

Tropic of Capricorn

Pitcairn
Island (UK)

Easter I.
(Chile)

La Paz
8.00am

Asunción

Brasília
9.00am

A R G E N T I N A

C
H
I
L
E

URUGUAY

Santiago

Buenos
Aires

Montevideo

Falkland Islands
(UK)

South Georgia
(UK)

Antarctic Circle

A B C D E

**Country names
numbered on map**

Europe
1 Albania
2 Andorra
3 Austria
4 Belgium
5 Bosnia-Herzegovina
6 Croatia
7 Czech Republic
8 Denmark
9 Estonia
10 Hungary
11 Kosovo
12 Latvia
13 Lithuania
14 Luxembourg
15 Macedonia
16 Moldova
17 Montenegro
18 Netherlands
19 Russian Federation
20 Serbia
21 Slovakia
22 Slovenia
23 Switzerland

Asia
24 Armenia
25 Azerbaijan
26 Georgia
27 Israel
28 Jordan
29 Lebanon
30 United Arab Emirates

Africa
31 Benin
32 Burkina
33 Burundi
34 Cameroon
35 Côte d'Ivoire
36 Equatorial Guinea
37 Ghana
38 Rwanda
39 Togo

South America
40 Guyana
41 Suriname

Total population
6829 million

Largest country
Russian Federation 17 075 400 sq km

Country with most people
China 1 330 265 000

Largest city
Tokyo 36 094 000

Key to symbols

Countries

■ Capital city

London
12.00 (noon)

The clocks show the time in a
selection of major world capital
cities when it is noon (Greenwich
Mean Time) in London.

0   800   1600   2400   3200 km

Scale : One centimetre on this map is the same as 800 kilometres on the ground.

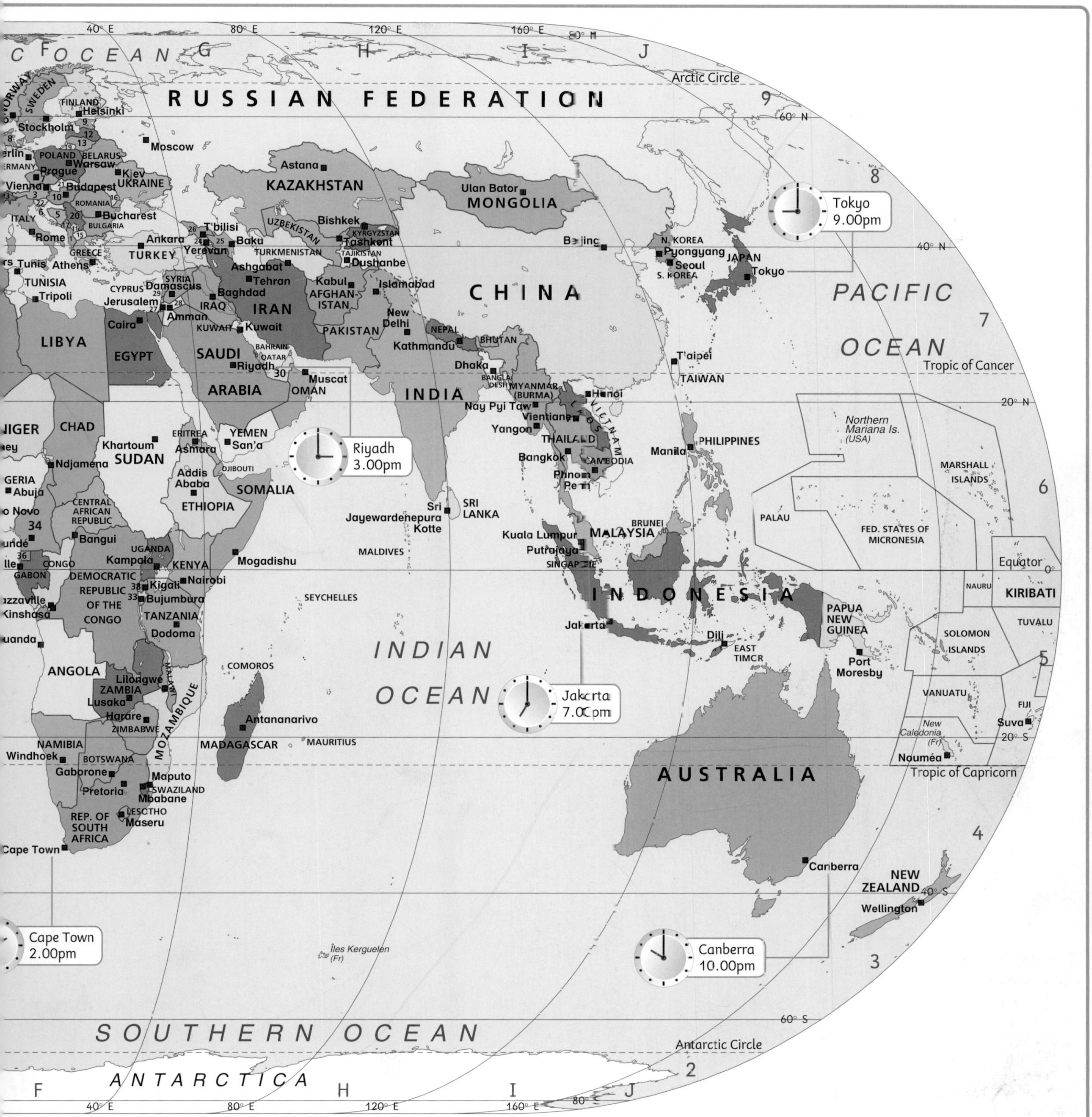

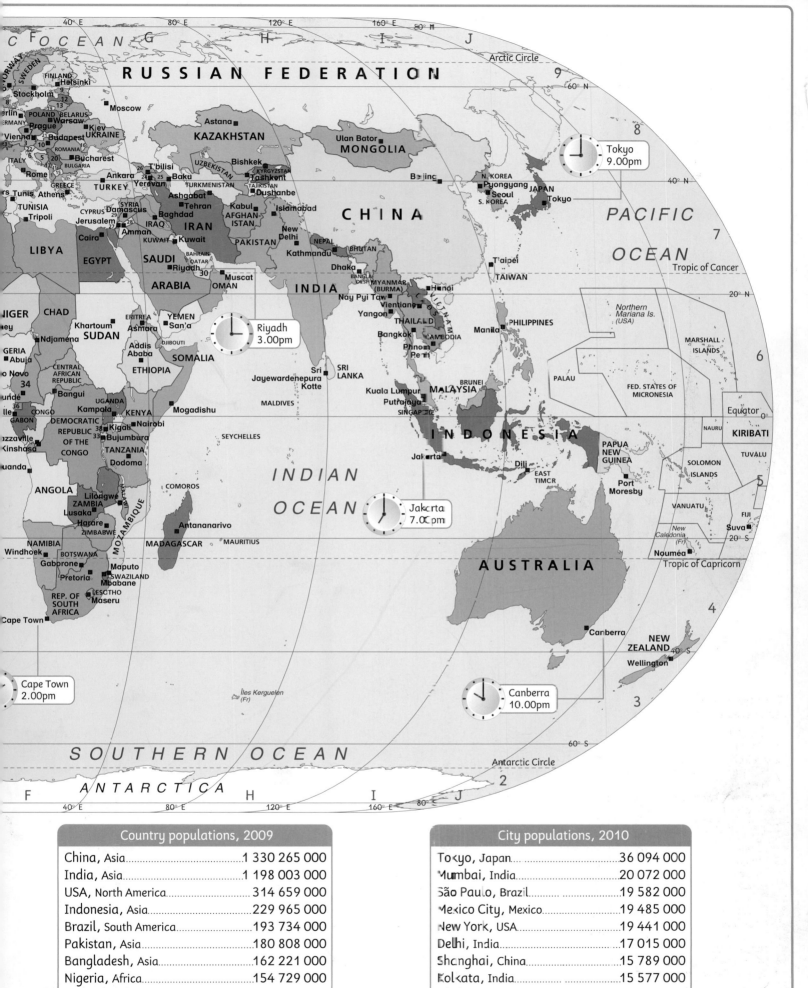

RUSSIAN FEDERATION
Arctic Circle
FINLAND
Helsinki
SWEDEN
Stockholm
Moscow
POLAND
BELARUS
Warsaw
Prague
Kiev
UKRAINE
Vienna
Budapest
ROMANIA
Bucharest
BULGARIA
ITALY
Rome
GREECE
Athens
Tunis
TUNISIA
Tripoli
LIBYA
Cairo
EGYPT
TURKEY
Ankara
T'bilisi
Baku
Yerevan
CYPRUS
SYRIA
Damascus
Jerusalem
Amman
IRAQ
Baghdad
IRAN
Tehran
KUWAIT
Kuwait
SAUDI ARABIA
Riyadh
BAHRAIN
QATAR
Muscat
OMAN
KAZAKHSTAN
Astana
UZBEKISTAN
TURKMENISTAN
Ashgabat
Bishkek
KYRGYZSTAN
Tashkent
TAJIKISTAN
Dushanbe
Kabul
AFGHANISTAN
Islamabad
PAKISTAN
New Delhi
INDIA
NEPAL
Kathmandu
BHUTAN
Dhaka
BANGLADESH
MONGOLIA
Ulan Bator
CHINA
N. KOREA
Pyongyang
Seoul
S. KOREA
JAPAN
Tokyo
Tokyo 9.00pm
PACIFIC OCEAN
Tropic of Cancer
T'aipei
TAIWAN
MYANMAR (BURMA)
Nay Pyi Taw
Yangon
Hanoi
Vientiane
THAILAND
Bangkok
CAMBODIA
VIETNAM
Manila
PHILIPPINES
Northern Mariana Is. (USA)
MARSHALL ISLANDS
PALAU
FED. STATES OF MICRONESIA
Equator
NAURU
KIRIBATI
TUVALU
CHAD
NIGER
NIGERIA
Abuja
Ndjamena
Khartoum
SUDAN
ERITREA
Asmara
YEMEN
San'a
DJIBOUTI
Addis Ababa
ETHIOPIA
SOMALIA
Riyadh 3.00pm
CENTRAL AFRICAN REPUBLIC
Bangui
CONGO
GABON
UGANDA
Kampala
KENYA
Nairobi
Mogadishu
DEMOCRATIC REPUBLIC OF THE CONGO
Kigali
Bujumbura
TANZANIA
Dodoma
Kinshasa
Luanda
ANGOLA
Lilongwe
MALAWI
ZAMBIA
Lusaka
Harare
ZIMBABWE
MOZAMBIQUE
NAMIBIA
Windhoek
BOTSWANA
Gaborone
Pretoria
Maputo
SWAZILAND
Mbabane
LESOTHO
Maseru
REP. OF SOUTH AFRICA
Cape Town
Cape Town 2.00pm
COMOROS
Antananarivo
MADAGASCAR
MAURITIUS
SEYCHELLES
MALDIVES
Sri Jayewardenepura Kotte
SRI LANKA
INDIAN OCEAN
Kuala Lumpur
Putrajaya
SINGAPORE
MALAYSIA
BRUNEI
INDONESIA
Jakarta
Dili
EAST TIMOR
Jakarta 7.00pm
PAPUA NEW GUINEA
Port Moresby
SOLOMON ISLANDS
VANUATU
FIJI
Suva
New Caledonia (Fr)
Nouméa
Tropic of Capricorn
AUSTRALIA
Canberra
Canberra 10.00pm
NEW ZEALAND
Wellington
Îles Kerguelen (Fr)
SOUTHERN OCEAN
Antarctic Circle
ANTARCTICA
40° E
80° E
120° E
160° E
60° N
40° N
20° N
0°
20° S
40° S
60° S

Country populations, 2009

China, Asia	1 330 265 000
India, Asia	1 198 003 000
USA, North America	314 659 000
Indonesia, Asia	229 965 000
Brazil, South America	193 734 000
Pakistan, Asia	180 808 000
Bangladesh, Asia	162 221 000
Nigeria, Africa	154 729 000
Russian Federation, Asia/Europe	140 874 000
Japan, Asia	127 156 000

City populations, 2010

Tokyo, Japan	36 094 000
Mumbai, India	20 072 000
São Paulo, Brazil	19 582 000
Mexico City, Mexico	19 485 000
New York, USA	19 441 000
Delhi, India	17 015 000
Shanghai, China	15 789 000
Kolkata, India	15 577 000
Dhaka, Bangladesh	14 796 000
Buenos Aires, Argentina	13 089 000

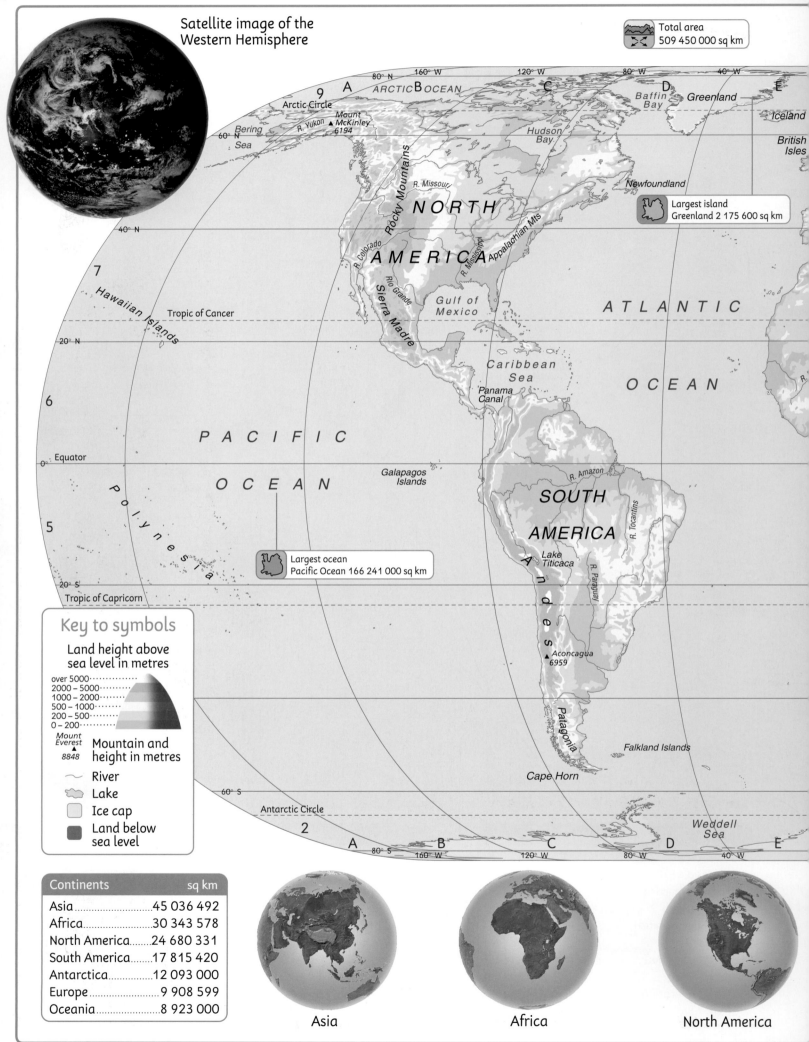

Satellite image of the
Western Hemisphere

Total area
509 450 000 sq km

Largest island
Greenland 2 175 600 sq km

Largest ocean
Pacific Ocean 166 241 000 sq km

ARCTIC OCEAN

Arctic Circle

Bering Sea

R. Yukon · Mount McKinley ▲ 6194

Baffin Bay · Greenland

Iceland

British Isles

Hudson Bay

Newfoundland

Rocky Mountains

R. Missouri

NORTH AMERICA

R. Colorado

R. Mississippi · Appalachian Mts

Sierra Madre

Rio Grande

Gulf of Mexico

ATLANTIC OCEAN

Tropic of Cancer

Caribbean Sea

Panama Canal

Hawaiian Islands

PACIFIC OCEAN

Equator

Galapagos Islands

R. Amazon

SOUTH AMERICA

R. Tocantins

Lake Titicaca

R. Paraguay

A n d e s

P o l y n e s i a

Tropic of Capricorn

▲ Aconcagua 6959

Patagonia

Falkland Islands

Cape Horn

Antarctic Circle

Weddell Sea

Key to symbols

Land height above sea level in metres

over 5000
2000 – 5000
1000 – 2000
500 – 1000
200 – 500
0 – 200

Mount Everest 8848 ▲ Mountain and height in metres

〜 River

Lake

Ice cap

Land below sea level

Continents	sq km
Asia	45 036 492
Africa	30 343 578
North America	24 680 331
South America	17 815 420
Antarctica	12 093 000
Europe	9 908 599
Oceania	8 923 000

Asia

Africa

North America

0 800 1600 2400 3200 km

Scale : One centimetre on this map is the same as 800 kilometres on the ground.

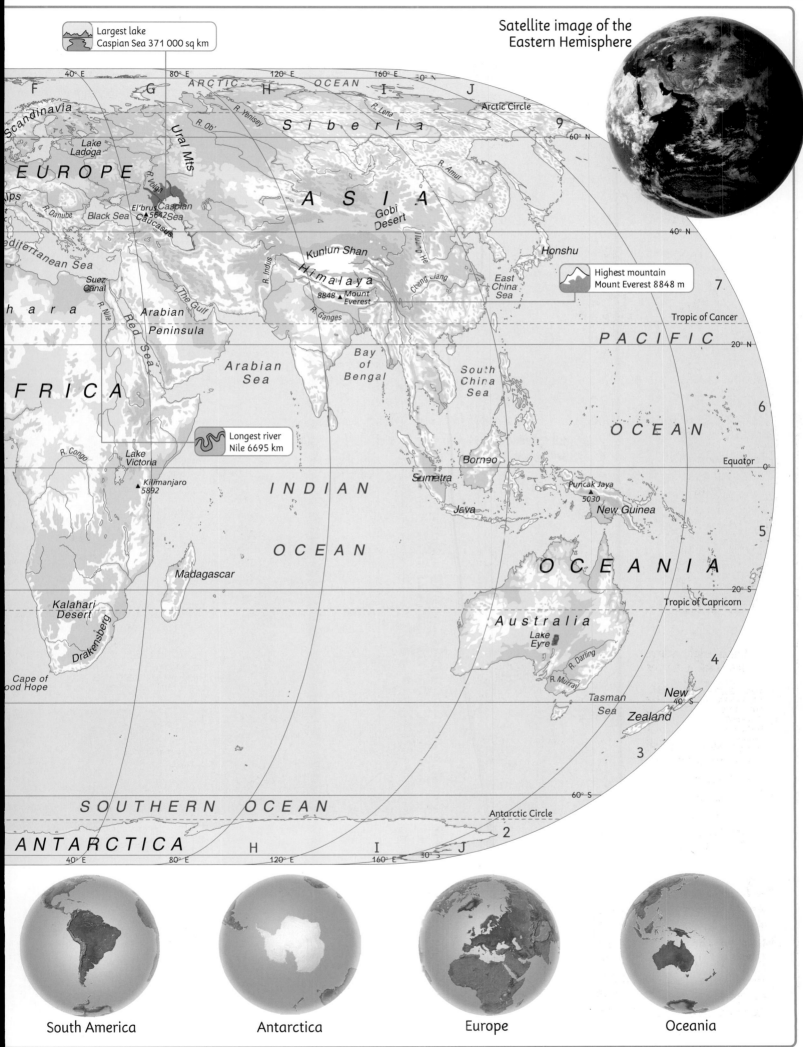

Satellite image of the Eastern Hemisphere

South America

Antarctica

Europe

Oceania

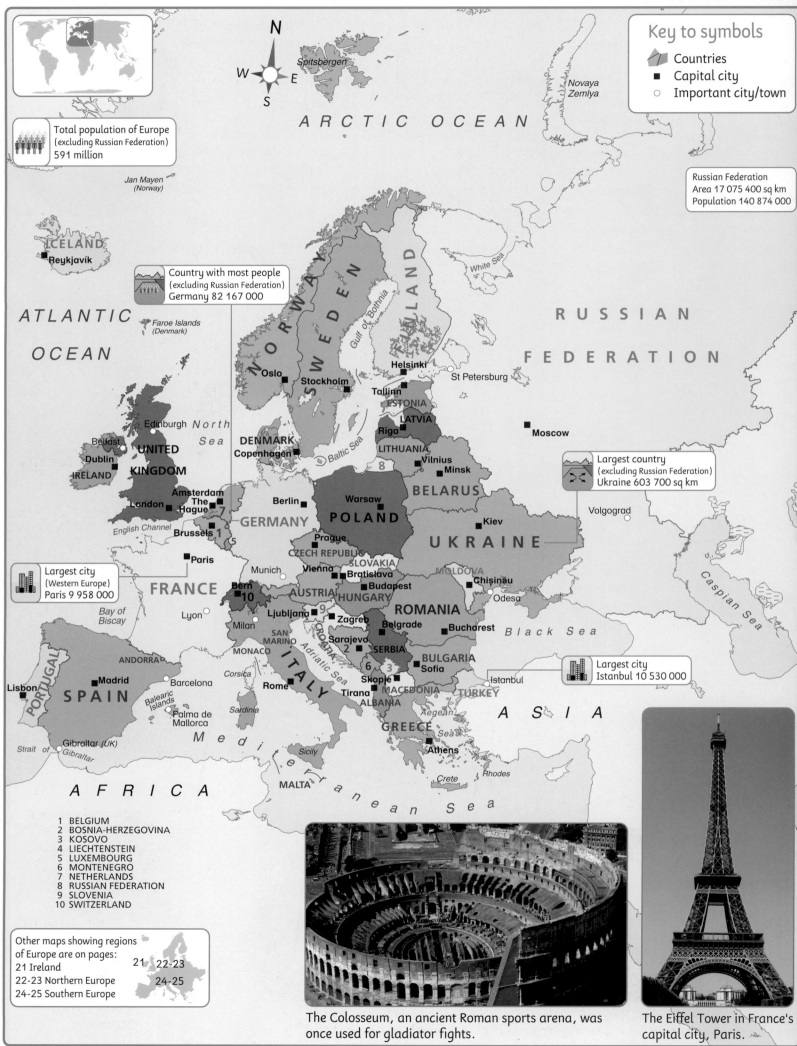

Key to symbols
- Countries
- ■ Capital city
- ○ Important city/town

Total population of Europe
(excluding Russian Federation)
591 million

Russian Federation
Area 17 075 400 sq km
Population 140 874 000

Country with most people
(excluding Russian Federation)
Germany 82 167 000

Largest country
(excluding Russian Federation)
Ukraine 603 700 sq km

Largest city
(Western Europe)
Paris 9 958 000

Largest city
Istanbul 10 530 000

ARCTIC OCEAN

Spitsbergen

Novaya
Zemlya

Jan Mayen
(Norway)

ATLANTIC OCEAN

Faroe Islands
(Denmark)

ICELAND
■ Reykjavík

RUSSIAN FEDERATION

White Sea

NORWAY
SWEDEN
FINLAND

Oslo
Stockholm
Helsinki
St Petersburg

Gulf of Bothnia

Tallinn
ESTONIA

Riga
LATVIA

Moscow

North Sea

Edinburgh

Belfast
UNITED KINGDOM
Dublin
IRELAND

DENMARK
Copenhagen

LITHUANIA
Vilnius
Minsk

Baltic Sea

8

BELARUS

Volgograd

London
Amsterdam
The Hague
7

Berlin

Warsaw
POLAND

Kiev

Brussels 1

GERMANY

Prague

UKRAINE

English Channel

5

CZECH REPUBLIC

Munich

SLOVAKIA
Vienna
Bratislava

MOLDOVA
Chișinău

Paris

Bern
10

AUSTRIA

Budapest
HUNGARY

Odesa

FRANCE

Lyon

Ljubljana
9

Zagreb

ROMANIA

Bucharest

Bay of Biscay

Milan
SAN MARINO
MONACO

CROATIA
Sarajevo
2

Belgrade
SERBIA

Black Sea

ANDORRA

ITALY

Adriatic Sea

6

3

BULGARIA
Sofia

Caspian Sea

PORTUGAL

Madrid

Barcelona

Corsica

Rome

Skopje
MACEDONIA

Istanbul

Lisbon

SPAIN

Balearic Islands

Palma de Mallorca

Sardinia

Tirana
ALBANIA

TURKEY

ASIA

Strait of Gibraltar

Gibraltar (UK)

GREECE

Aegean Sea

Athens

Mediterranean Sea

Sicily

MALTA

Crete

Rhodes

AFRICA

1 BELGIUM
2 BOSNIA-HERZEGOVINA
3 KOSOVO
4 LIECHTENSTEIN
5 LUXEMBOURG
6 MONTENEGRO
7 NETHERLANDS
8 RUSSIAN FEDERATION
9 SLOVENIA
10 SWITZERLAND

Other maps showing regions
of Europe are on pages:
21 Ireland
22-23 Northern Europe
24-25 Southern Europe

21 22-23
24-25

The Colosseum, an ancient Roman sports arena, was
once used for gladiator fights.

The Eiffel Tower in France's
capital city, Paris.

0 250 500 750 1000 1250 km

Scale : One centimetre on this map is the same as 250 kilometres on the ground.

Mount Etna, on the island of Sicily, is one of the world's most active volcanoes.

Narrow, steep sided inlets called fjords are found along much of the Norwegian coastline.

Key to symbols

Land height above sea level in metres

over 5000
2000 – 5000
1000 – 2000
500 – 1000
200 – 500
0 – 200

El'brus
▲
5642   Mountain and height in metres

∼   River

Lake

Seasonal lake

Ice cap

Land below sea level

Largest island
Great Britain 218 476 sq km

Total area of Europe
9 908 599 sq km

Longest river
Volga 3688 km

Largest lake
Caspian Sea 371 000 sq km

Highest mountain
El'brus 5642 m

Scale : One centimetre on this map s the same as 250 kilometres on the ground.

250   500   750   1000   1250 km

European Union

The European Union (EU) was created in 1957 by the Treaty of Rome. The original members of the then European Economic Community (EEC) were Belgium, France, West Germany, Italy, Luxembourg and the Netherlands. Since 1957 the EU has grown and now has 27 member states. The total population of the EU is now nearly half a billion.

The headquarters of the EU in the Belgian capital, Brussels.

EU member
EU applicant
Non EU member

B.-H.   BOSNIA-HERZEGOVINA
KOS.   KOSOVO
L.   LIECHTENSTEIN
LUX.   LUXEMBOURG
MAC.   MACEDONIA
MOL.   MOLDOVA
MON.   MONTENEGRO
R.F.   RUSSIAN FEDERATION
SL.   SLOVENIA
SWITZ.   SWITZERLAND

ICELAND

NORWAY
SWEDEN
FINLAND
ESTONIA
LATVIA
LITHUANIA
R.F.
DENMARK
UNITED KINGDOM
IRELAND
NETHERLANDS
BELGIUM
LUX.
GERMANY
POLAND
BELARUS
UKRAINE
CZECH REPUBLIC
SLOVAKIA
FRANCE
SWITZ.
L.
AUSTRIA
HUNGARY
MOL.
SL.
CROATIA
ROMANIA
B.-H.
SERBIA
MON.
KOS.
MAC.
BULGARIA
ALBANIA
ANDORRA
ITALY
PORTUGAL
SPAIN
GREECE
TURKEY
MALTA
CYPRUS

Austria
Belgium
Bulgaria
Cyprus
Czech Republic
Denmark
Estonia
Finland
France
Germany
Greece
Hungary
Ireland
Italy
Latvia
Lithuania
Luxembourg
Malta
Netherlands
Poland
Portugal
Romania
Slovakia
Slovenia
Spain
Sweden
United Kingdom

Key to symbols

- Countries
- ■ Capital city
- ○ Important city/town

Other maps showing regions of the
United Kingdom are on pages:
18-19 England and Wales
20 Scotland
21 Northern Ireland

N W E S

Shetland Islands

Orkney Islands

ATLANTIC OCEAN

Outer Hebrides

Inverness

Aberdeen

Fort William

SCOTLAND

Dundee

North Sea

Glasgow   ■ Edinburgh

Londonderry

NORTHERN IRELAND   ■ Belfast

UNITED

Newcastle upon Tyne

Middlesbrough

Dundalk

Isle of Man

York

IRELAND

Blackpool   Bradford   Leeds
Preston

Irish Sea

Manchester
Liverpool   Sheffield

Galway

Dublin ■

KINGDOM

Stoke-on-Trent   Derby   Nottingham

ENGLAND   Norwich

Limerick

Wolverhampton   Leicester
Birmingham

WALES   Coventry

Cambridge   Ipswich

Waterford

Cork

Oxford   London ■   Southend-on-Sea

Swansea

Bristol   Reading

BELGIUM

Cardiff ■

Celtic Sea

Southampton   Brighton
Portsmouth
Bournemouth

Plymouth   Torquay

English Channel

Channel Islands

FRANCE

Tower Bridge crosses the River Thames in London.

50   100   150   200   250 km

Scale : One centimetre on this map is the same as 50 kilometres on the ground.

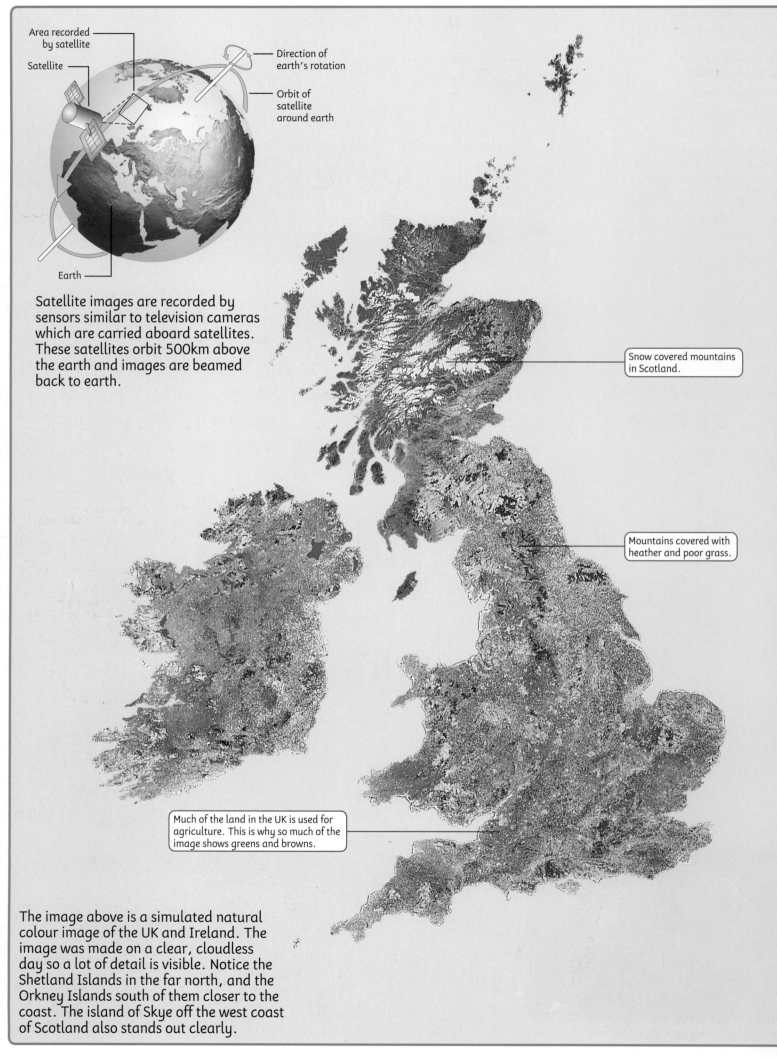

Area recorded by satellite

Satellite

Direction of earth's rotation

Orbit of satellite around earth

Earth

Satellite images are recorded by sensors similar to television cameras which are carried aboard satellites. These satellites orbit 500km above the earth and images are beamed back to earth.

Snow covered mountains in Scotland.

Mountains covered with heather and poor grass.

Much of the land in the UK is used for agriculture. This is why so much of the image shows greens and browns.

The image above is a simulated natural colour image of the UK and Ireland. The image was made on a clear, cloudless day so a lot of detail is visible. Notice the Shetland Islands in the far north, and the Orkney Islands south of them closer to the coast. The island of Skye off the west coast of Scotland also stands out clearly.

Key to symbols

Land height above sea level in metres

- over 1000
- 500 – 1000
- 200 – 500
- 100 – 200
- 0 – 100

▲ *Ben Nevis* **1344** Mountain and height in metres

〜 River

▱ Lake

▮ Land below sea level

Total area of the United Kingdom
244 082 sq km

Largest lake
Lough Neagh 396 sq km

Highest mountain
Ben Nevis 1344 m

Largest island
Great Britain 218 476 sq km

Longest river
River Severn 354 km

One of Scotland's famous glens, Glencoe.

The South Downs drop down to the sea in chalk cliffs at Beachy Head.

N
W E
S

Shetland Islands
Mainland
Sumburgh Head

Orkney Islands
Mainland
Hoy
Pentland Firth
Duncansby Head

Cape Wrath

Outer Hebrides
Isle of Lewis
Harris
St Kilda
North Uist
South Uist
Skye
Inner Hebrides
Rum
Coll
Tiree
Mull
Ben More 966
Jura
Islay
Arran

The Minch

North West Highlands
Loch Ness
Ben Nevis 1344 ▲
Glen Coe
Morey Firth
R. Spey
Cairngorm Mts
Ben Macdui 1309 ▲
R. Dee
Grampian Mts
Loch Tay
Loch Lomond
R. Tay
Ochil Hills
R. Forth
Firth of Forth
Firth of Clyde

ATLANTIC OCEAN

Malin Head
Donegal Bay
Achill
Lough Mask
Lough Corrib
Galway Bay
R. Foyle
Lower Lough Erne
Upper Lough Erne
R. Shannon
Lough Ree
Lough Derg
R. Barrow
R. Shannon
R. Suir
Carrantuohill 1041 ▲
R. Blackwater
Cape Clear

Ireland

Lough Neagh
Antrim Hills
R. Bann
Mourne Mts
Slieve Donard 852 ▲
Dundalk Bay
R. Boyne
Lugnaquilla Mtn 926 ▲
Wicklow Mts

North Channel

Southern Uplands
Merrick 843
R. Tweed
Cheviot Hills
R. Tyne
R. Tees
Scafell Pike 977 ▲
Lake District
Soway Firth
R. Crede

Great Britain

North York Moors
Flamborough Head
Spurn Head

Pennines

Isle of Man
Irish Sea
R. Ouse
High Peak
R. Mersey
Kinder Scout 636
R. Trent
The Wash

Anglesey
Snowdon 1085 ▲
R. Dee
Cambrian Mountains
Cardigan Bay
R. Severn
Black Mountains 886 ▲
Brecon Beacons
R. Wye
Cotswold Hills
R. Thames
Chiltern Hills
R. Thames
R. Avon
R. Great Ouse
The Fens
Norfolk Broads

St George's Channel
St David's Head

Celtic Sea

Land's End
Isles of Scilly
Bodmin Moor
R. Tamar
Dartmoor
Yes Tor 615 ▲
Start Point
Lyme Bay
Exmoor
Bristol Channel
Mendip Hills
South Downs
North Downs
Isle of Wight
Beachy Head

English Channel

Channel Islands

North Sea

Scale : One centimetre on this map is the same as 50 kilometres on the ground.

50 100 150 200 250 km

In this year...

Cardiff becomes the capital city of Wales.

Channel Tunnel is opened.

The worst floods for 60 years hit central England.

London will host the Olympic Games.

1955	
1994	
2007	
2012	

North Sea

Norfolk Broads

The Wash

Irish Sea

North Channel

Isle of Man

Firth of Clyde

Solway Firth

Morecambe Bay

SCOTLAND

NORTHERN IRELAND

IRELAND

ENGLAND

Pennines

Southern Uplands

Cheviot Hills

North York Moors

Lake District

Ochil Hills

High Peak

Anglesey

Caernarfon Bay

N E S W

Scale : One centimetre on this map is the same as 20 kilometres on the ground.

0   20   40   60   80   100 km

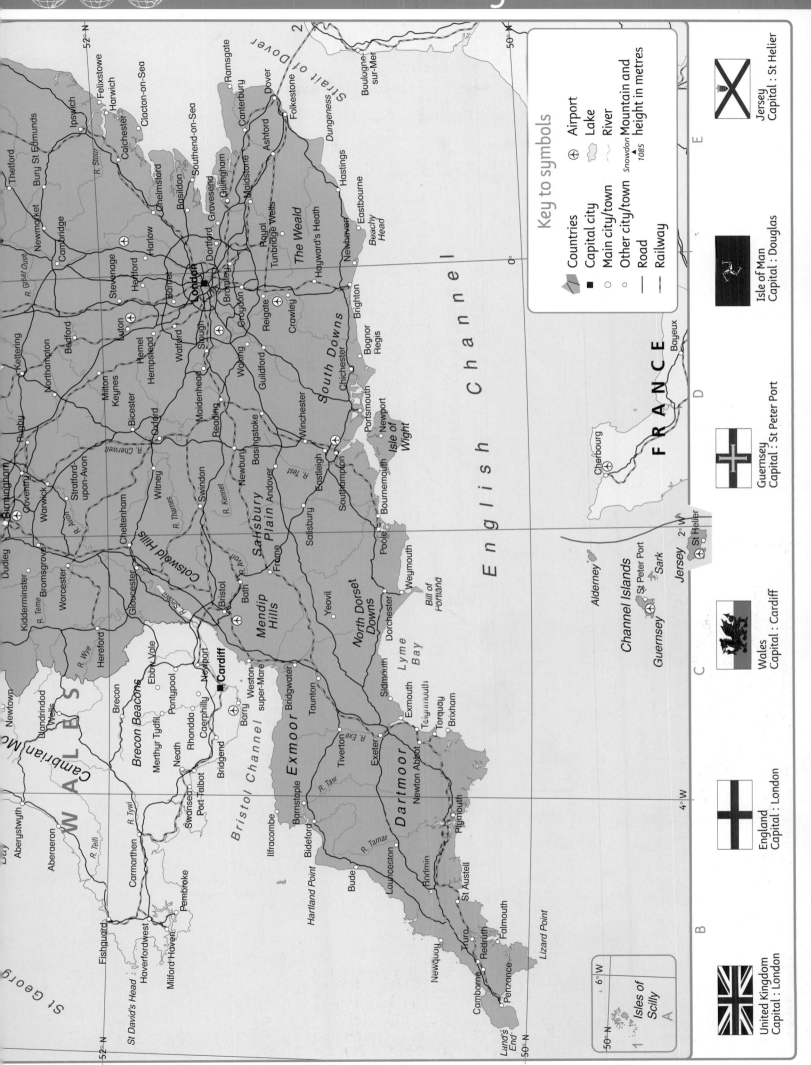

Key to symbols

Countries
Capital city
Main city/town
Other city/town
Road
Railway

Airport
Lake
River
Snowdon Mountain and
▲1085 height in metres

United Kingdom
Capital : London

England
Capital : London

Wales
Capital : Cardiff

Guernsey
Capital : St Peter Port

Isle of Man
Capital : Douglas

Jersey
Capital : St Helier

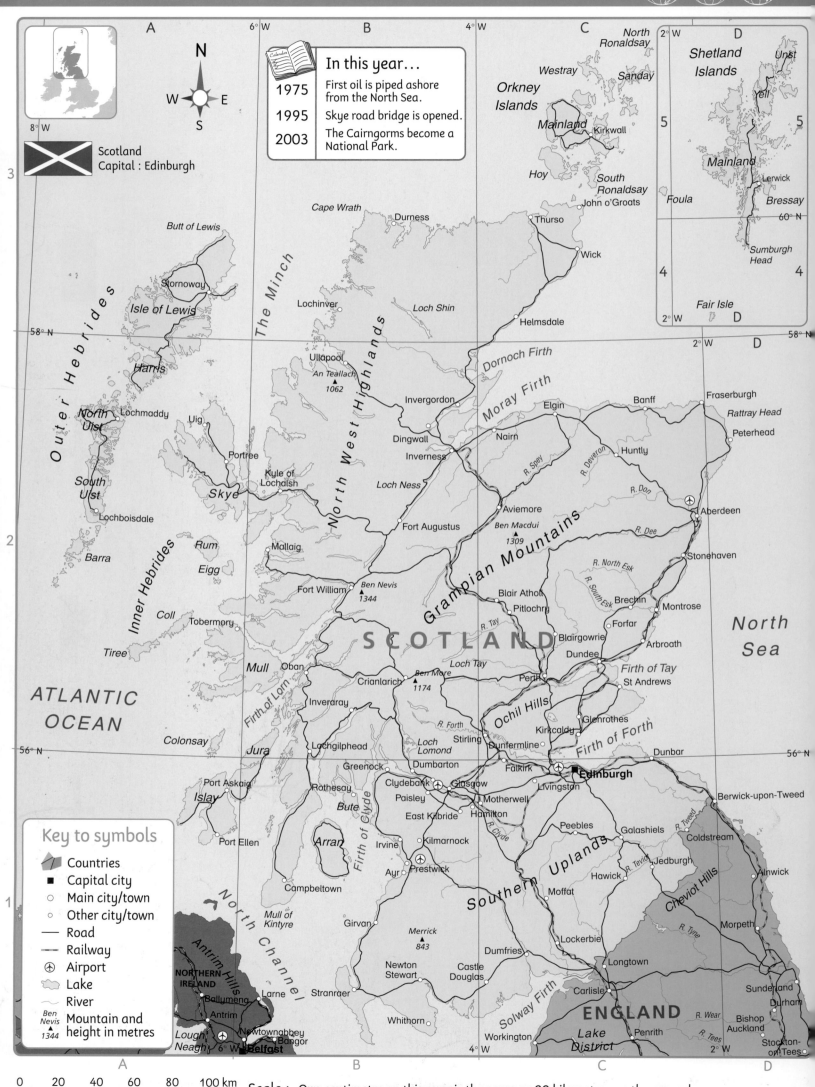

20 Scotland

In this year...

1975 — First oil is piped ashore from the North Sea.

1995 — Skye road bridge is opened.

2003 — The Cairngorms become a National Park.

Scotland
Capital : Edinburgh

Key to symbols

- Countries
- ■ Capital city
- ○ Main city/town
- ○ Other city/town
- — Road
- —⊢ Railway
- ✈ Airport
- Lake
- River
- *Ben Nevis* ▲ *1344* Mountain and height in metres

Scale : One centimetre on this map is the same as 20 kilometres on the ground.

0 20 40 60 80 100 km

Orkney Islands — North Ronaldsay, Westray, Sanday, Mainland, Kirkwall, Hoy, South Ronaldsay, John o'Groats

Shetland Islands — Unst, Yell, Mainland, Foula, Lerwick, Bressay, Sumburgh Head, Fair Isle

ATLANTIC OCEAN

Outer Hebrides — Butt of Lewis, Stornoway, Isle of Lewis, Harris, North Uist, Lochmaddy, South Uist, Lochboisdale, Barra

Inner Hebrides — Uig, Portree, Skye, Kyle of Lochalsh, Rum, Eigg, Coll, Tobermory, Tiree, Mull, Colonsay, Jura, Islay, Port Askaig, Port Ellen

The Minch

Cape Wrath, Durness, Thurso, Wick, Helmsdale

Lochinver, Loch Shin, Ullapool, An Teallach 1062, North West Highlands, Dornoch Firth, Moray Firth, Invergordon, Elgin, Banff, Fraserburgh, Rattray Head, Peterhead, Dingwall, Nairn, Inverness, Huntly, Loch Ness, R. Spey, R. Deveron, R. Don, Aberdeen, Aviemore, Ben Macdui 1309, Grampian Mountains, R. Dee, Stonehaven

Fort Augustus, Mallaig, Fort William, Ben Nevis 1344, Blair Atholl, Pitlochry, R. North Esk, R. South Esk, Brechin, Montrose, Forfar, Arbroath, R. Tay, Blairgowrie, Dundee

SCOTLAND

North Sea

Oban, Crianlarich, Ben More 1174, Loch Tay, Perth, St Andrews, Firth of Tay, Inveraray, Firth of Lorn, R. Forth, Ochil Hills, Glenrothes, Lochgilphead, Loch Lomond, Stirling, Kirkcaldy, Firth of Forth, Dunfermline, Dunbar, Greenock, Dumbarton, Falkirk, Livingston, Edinburgh, Clydebank, Glasgow, Motherwell, Berwick-upon-Tweed, Paisley, East Kilbride, Hamilton, R. Clyde, Firth of Clyde, Rothesay, Bute, Arran, Irvine, Kilmarnock, Peebles, Galashiels, R. Tweed, Coldstream, Ayr, Prestwick, Hawick, R. Teviot, Jedburgh, Cheviot Hills, Alnwick, Campbeltown, Mull of Kintyre, Girvan, Merrick 843, Southern Uplands, Moffat, Lockerbie, Morpeth, R. Tyne

North Channel, Larne, Stranraer, Newton Stewart, Castle Douglas, Dumfries, Longtown, Sunderland, Durham, Bishop Auckland, Stockton-on-Tees

NORTHERN IRELAND, Antrim Hills, Ballymena, Antrim, Newtownabbey, Bangor, Belfast, Lough Neagh

Solway Firth, Carlisle, Workington, Whithorn, ENGLAND, Lake District, Penrith, R. Wear, R. Tees, Longtown

Key to symbols

- Countries
- ■ Capital city
- ○ Main city/town
- ○ Other city/town
- — Road
- ┄ Railway
- ⊕ Airport
- Lake
- River
- *Carrantuohill* ▲ 1041 Mountain and height in metres

In this year...

1920 Ireland becomes an independent country.

2002 Ireland adopts the euro as its currency.

2005 Ireland's first offshore wind farm is switched on at Arklow Bank.

Ireland
Capital : Dublin

Northern Ireland
Capital : Belfast

Scale : One centimetre on this map is the same as 20 kilometres on the ground.

0 20 40 60 80 100 km

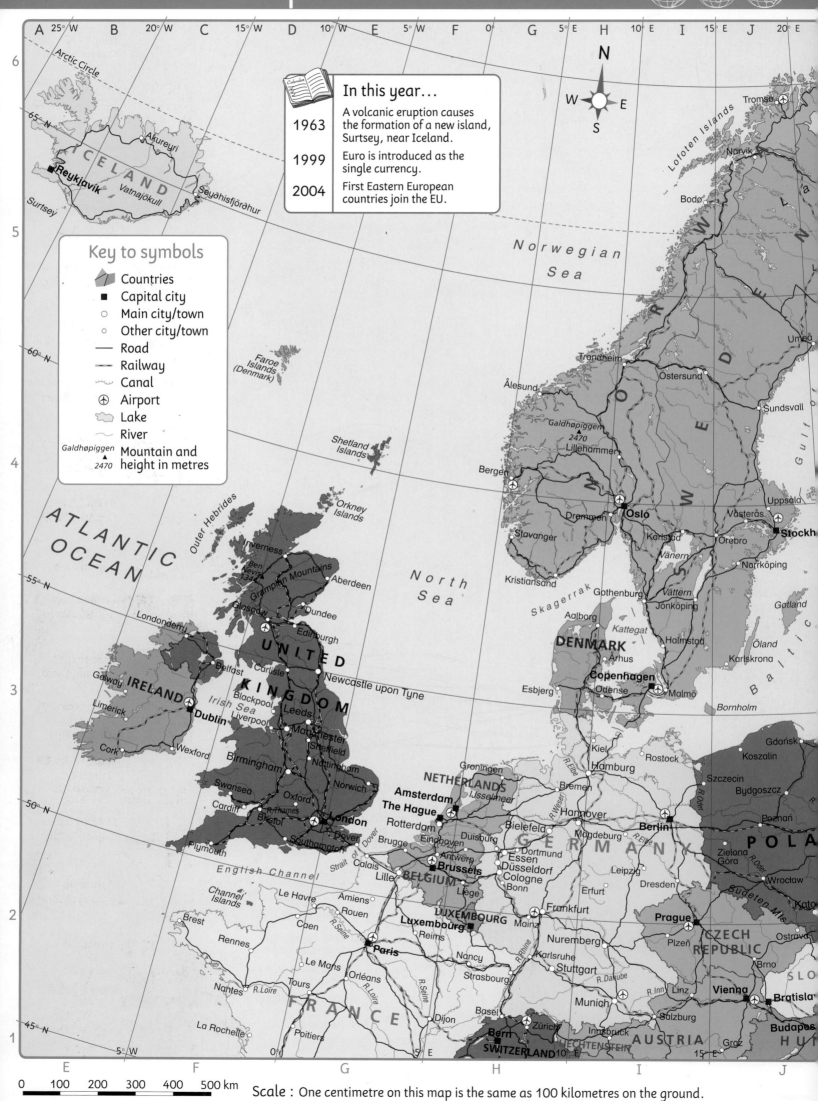

A 25° W   B 20° W   C 15° W   D 10° W   E 5° W   F 0°   G 5° E   H 10° E   I 15° E   J 20° E

In this year...

1963 — A volcanic eruption causes the formation of a new island, Surtsey, near Iceland.

1999 — Euro is introduced as the single currency.

2004 — First Eastern European countries join the EU.

Key to symbols

- Countries
- ■ Capital city
- ○ Main city/town
- ○ Other city/town
- — Road
- ⊢⊢ Railway
- 〜 Canal
- ⊕ Airport
- ▨ Lake
- 〜 River
- *Galdhøpiggen* ▲ 2470 — Mountain and height in metres

Arctic Circle

65° N

ICELAND
Akureyri
■ Reykjavík
Vatnajökull
Seyðisfjörður
Surtsey

60° N

ATLANTIC OCEAN

55° N

Faroe Islands (Denmark)

Shetland Islands

Outer Hebrides

Orkney Islands
Inverness
Ben Nevis 1344
Grampian Mountains
Aberdeen
Glasgow
Dundee
Edinburgh

Londonderry
Belfast
Carlisle
Newcastle upon Tyne

IRELAND
Galway
Limerick
Cork
Wexford

Irish Sea
Blackpool
Liverpool
Manchester
Sheffield
Leeds
Nottingham

UNITED KINGDOM

50° N

Dublin ■
Birmingham
Swansea
Cardiff
Bristol
Oxford
R. Thames
London
Norwich

Channel Islands
Brest
Rennes
Nantes
R. Loire
La Rochelle
Poitiers
Le Mans
Tours
Orléans

Plymouth
English Channel
Strait of Dover
Dover
Southampton
Calais
Lille
Brugge

Le Havre
Amiens
Rouen
Caen
R. Seine
Reims

45° N

FRANCE

Paris ■
Nancy
Strasbourg
R. Rhine
Karlsruhe
Basel
Dijon
Zürich

Norwegian Sea

North Sea

N W R A

Tromsø
Lofoten Islands
Narvik
Bodø

Trondheim
Ålesund
Galdhøpiggen 2470
Lillehammer
Bergen
Oslo ■
Drammen
Stavanger
Kristiansand

Skagerrak

SWEDEN

Östersund
Sundsvall
Umeå

Karlstad
Vänern
Örebro
Uppsala
Västerås
Stockholm ■
Norrköping
Jönköping
Vättern
Gotland

DENMARK
Gothenburg
Aalborg
Kattegat
Halmstad
Öland
Karlskrona
Århus
Copenhagen ■
Esbjerg
Odense
Malmö
Bornholm

Baltic

Kiel
Rostock
Gdańsk
Koszalin
Szczecin
Bydgoszcz

NETHERLANDS
Groningen
Amsterdam ■
The Hague
Rotterdam
IJsselmeer
Eindhoven
Antwerp
BELGIUM
Brussels ■
Liège

R. Elbe
Hamburg
Bremen
Bielefeld
Hannover
R. Weser
Magdeburg
Berlin ■

POLA
Zielona Góra
Poznań
R. Oder
Wrocław

Duisburg
Dortmund
Essen
Düsseldorf
Cologne
Bonn

GERMANY

Leipzig
Erfurt
Dresden

Sudeten Mts

LUXEMBOURG
Luxembourg ■
Mainz
Frankfurt
Nuremberg
Plzeň
Prague ■
CZECH REPUBLIC
Brno

R. Rhine
R. Danube
Stuttgart
R. Inn
Munich
Linz
Salzburg
Innsbruck
AUSTRIA
Vienna ■
Bratislava ■
SLO

Bern ■
SWITZERLAND
LIECHTENSTEIN

Budapes
HU

E 5° W   F 0°   G 5° E   H 10° E   I 15° E   J

0   100   200   300   400   500 km

Scale : One centimetre on this map is the same as 100 kilometres on the ground.

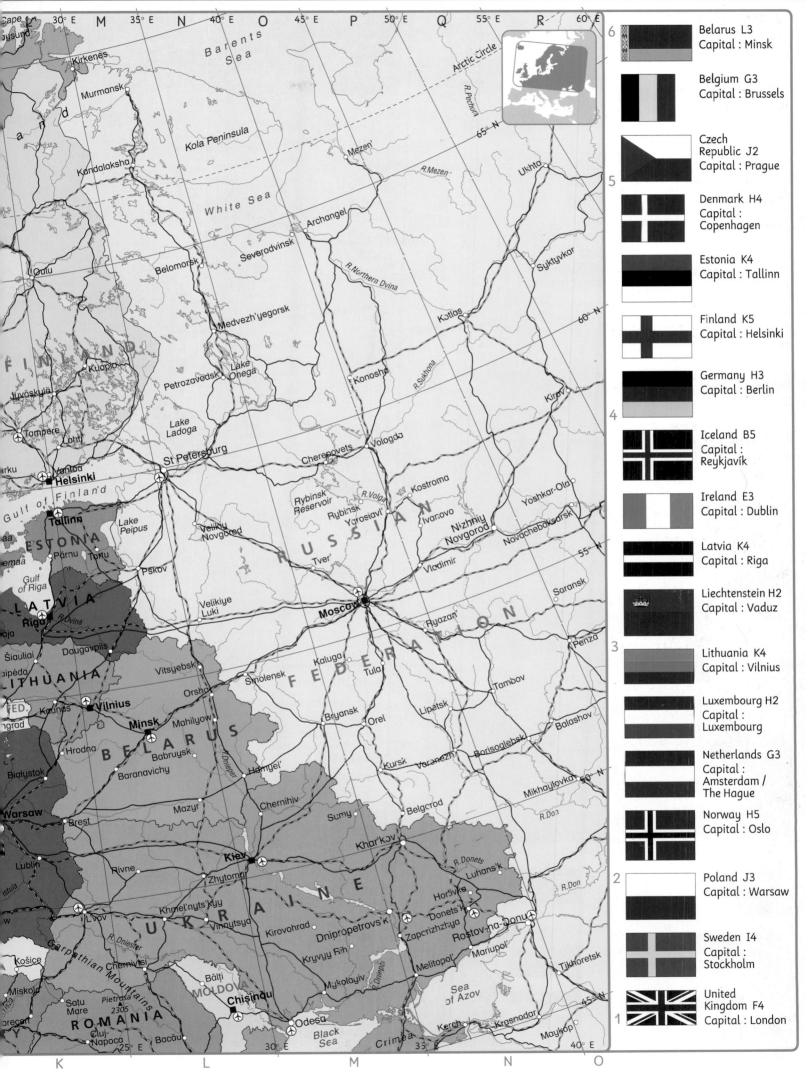

Map Labels

Seas and Waters: Barents Sea, White Sea, Gulf of Finland, Gulf of Riga, Lake Peipus, Lake Ladoga, Lake Onega, Rybinsk Reservoir, Black Sea, Sea of Azov

Rivers: R. Pechora, R. Mezen, R. Northern Dvina, R. Sukhona, R. Volga, R. Dvina, R. Dnieper, R. Dniester, R. Don, R. Donets

Countries: FINLAND, RUSSIAN FEDERATION, ESTONIA, LATVIA, LITHUANIA, BELARUS, UKRAINE, MOLDOVA, ROMANIA, POLAND

Cities: Kirkenes, Murmansk, Kandalaksha, Oulu, Belomorsk, Severodvinsk, Archangel, Mezen', Ukhta, Syktyvkar, Kotlas, Medvezh'yegorsk, Konosha, Kirov, Petrozavodsk, Vologda, Cherepovets, Kostroma, Yoshkar-Ola, Kuopio, Jyväskylä, Tampere, Lohja, Vantaa, Helsinki, St Petersburg, Rybinsk, Yaroslavl', Ivanovo, Nizhniy Novgorod, Novacheboksarsk, Tallinn, Pärnu, Tartu, Pskov, Velikiy Novgorod, Tver', Vladimir, Saransk, Riga, Daugavpils, Velikiye Luki, Moscow, Šiauliai, Vitsyebsk, Smolensk, Kaluga, Tula, Ryazan', Penza, Vilnius, Kaunas, Minsk, Mahilyow, Orsha, Bryansk, Orel, Lipetsk, Tambov, Balashov, Hrodna, Babruysk, Homyel', Kursk, Voronezh, Borisoglebsk, Białystok, Baranavichy, Chernihiv, Sumy, Belgorod, Mikhaylovka, Warsaw, Brest, Mazyr, Kiev, Khar'kov, Lublin, Rivne, Zhytomyr, R. Donets, Luhans'k, L'vov, Khmel'nyts'kyy, Vinnytsya, Kirovohrad, Dnipropetrovs'k, Horlivka, Donets'k, Rostov-na-Donu, Košice, Bălţi, Zaporizhzhya, Mariupol', Satu Mare, Pietrasa 2305, Chişinău, Kryvyy Rih, Melitopol', Mykolayiv, Tikhoretsk, Miskolc, Cluj-Napoca, Bacău, ROMANIA, Odesa, Kerch, Crimea, Krasnodar, Maykop

Other labels: Kola Peninsula, Arctic Circle, Carpathian Mountains

Coordinates: 30°E, 35°E, 40°E, 45°E, 50°E, 55°E, 60°E, 65°N, 60°N, 55°N, 50°N, 45°N, 25°E, 33°E, 40°E

Legend

Country	Ref	Capital
Belarus	L3	Minsk
Belgium	G3	Brussels
Czech Republic	J2	Prague
Denmark	H4	Copenhagen
Estonia	K4	Tallinn
Finland	K5	Helsinki
Germany	H3	Berlin
Iceland	B5	Reykjavík
Ireland	E3	Dublin
Latvia	K4	Riga
Liechtenstein	H2	Vaduz
Lithuania	K4	Vilnius
Luxembourg	H2	Luxembourg
Netherlands	G3	Amsterdam / The Hague
Norway	H5	Oslo
Poland	J3	Warsaw
Sweden	I4	Stockholm
United Kingdom	F4	London

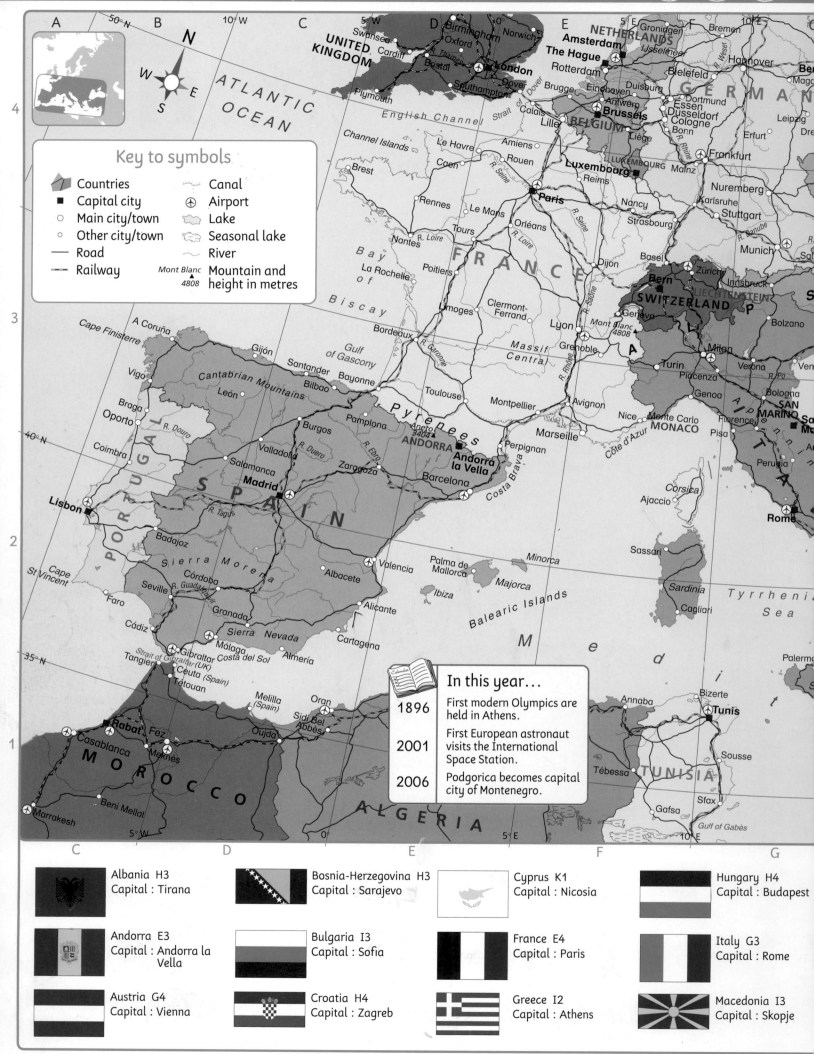

Key to symbols

- Countries
- Capital city
- Main city/town
- Other city/town
- Road
- Railway
- Canal
- Airport
- Lake
- Seasonal lake
- River
- Mont Blanc 4808 ▲ Mountain and height in metres

In this year...

1896 First modern Olympics are held in Athens.

2001 First European astronaut visits the International Space Station.

2006 Podgorica becomes capital city of Montenegro.

Albania H3 Capital : Tirana

Andorra E3 Capital : Andorra la Vella

Austria G4 Capital : Vienna

Bosnia-Herzegovina H3 Capital : Sarajevo

Bulgaria I3 Capital : Sofia

Croatia H4 Capital : Zagreb

Cyprus K1 Capital : Nicosia

France E4 Capital : Paris

Greece I2 Capital : Athens

Hungary H4 Capital : Budapest

Italy G3 Capital : Rome

Macedonia I3 Capital : Skopje

0 100 200 300 400 500 km

Scale : One centimetre on this map is the same as 100 kilometres on the ground.

Malta **G2**
Capital : Valletta

Portugal **C2**
Capital : Lisbon

Slovakia **H4**
Capital : Bratislava

Switzerland **F4**
Capital : Bern

Moldova **J4**
Capital : Chişinău

Romania **I4**
Capital : Bucharest

Slovenia **G4**
Capital : Ljubljana

Turkey **J2**
Capital : Ankara

Montenegro **H3**
Capital : Podgorica

Serbia **I3**
Capital : Belgrade

Spain **C3**
Capital : Madrid

Ukraine **J4**
Capital : Kiev

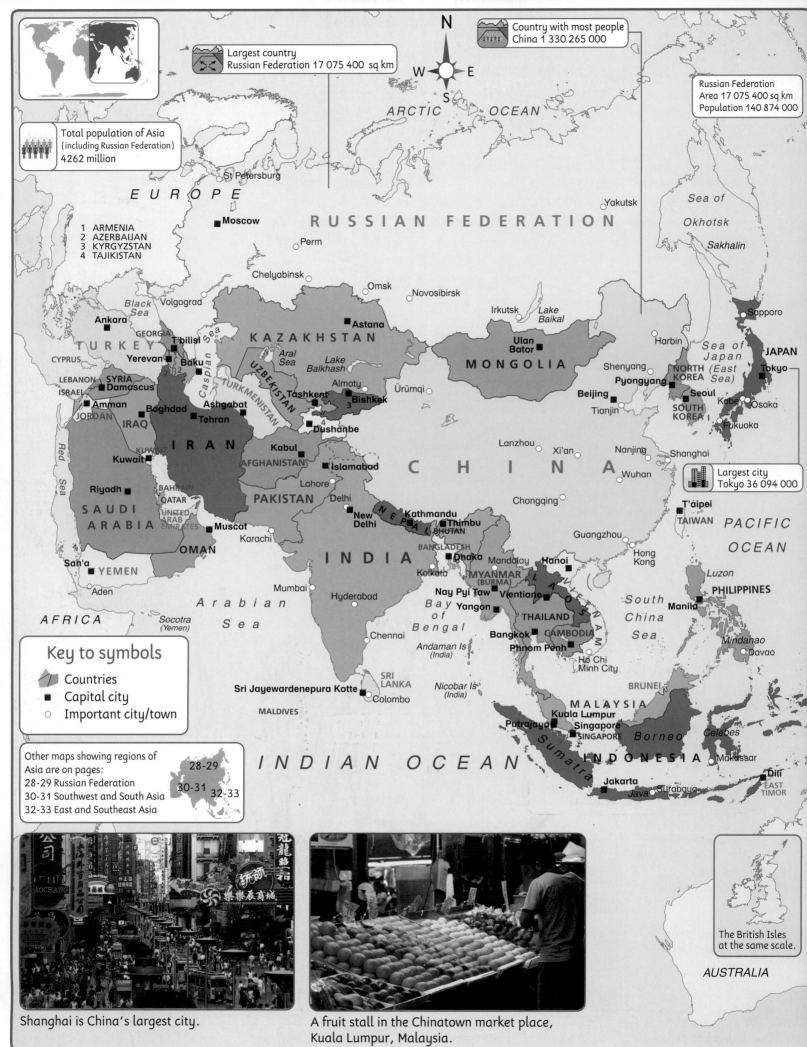

Largest country
Russian Federation 17 075 400 sq km

Country with most people
China 1 330 265 000

Russian Federation
Area 17 075 400 sq km
Population 140 874 000

Total population of Asia
(including Russian Federation)
4262 million

1 ARMENIA
2 AZERBAIJAN
3 KYRGYZSTAN
4 TAJIKISTAN

ARCTIC OCEAN

EUROPE

St Petersburg

Yakutsk

RUSSIAN FEDERATION

Sea of Okhotsk

Moscow

Sakhalin

Perm

Chelyabinsk

Omsk
Novosibirsk

Irkutsk
Lake Baikal

Sapporo

Black Sea

Volgograd

Ankara

Astana

KAZAKHSTAN

Ulan Bator

MONGOLIA

Harbin

Sea of Japan (East Sea)

JAPAN

GEORGIA

T'bilisi

Caspian Sea

Aral Sea

Lake Balkhash

Shenyang

Tokyo

CYPRUS
TURKEY

Yerevan

Baku

UZBEKISTAN

Almaty

Ürümqi

NORTH KOREA
Pyongyang

LEBANON
SYRIA
ISRAEL
Damascus

Tashkent

Bishkek

Beijing

SOUTH KOREA

Seoul

Kobe
Osaka

TURKMENISTAN

Amman
JORDAN
Baghdad
IRAQ

Ashgabat
Dushanbe

Tianjin

Fukuoka

Tehran

Lanzhou

Xi'an

Nanjing

Shanghai

Kuwait

IRAN

Kabul

CHINA

Wuhan

Largest city
Tokyo 36 094 000

Riyadh

AFGHANISTAN

Islamabad

Chongqing

T'aipei

BAHRAIN
QATAR

Lahore

PAKISTAN

Delhi

NEPAL

Kathmandu

TAIWAN

PACIFIC OCEAN

SAUDI ARABIA

UNITED ARAB EMIRATES

New Delhi

Thimbu
BHUTAN

Guangzhou

Muscat

Karachi

BANGLADESH

Hong Kong

San'a

OMAN

INDIA

Dhaka

Mandalay

Hanoi

Luzon

YEMEN

Mumbai

Hyderabad

Kolkata

MYANMAR (BURMA)

LAOS

PHILIPPINES

Aden

Nay Pyi Taw

Vientiane

South China Sea

Manila

AFRICA

Socotra (Yemen)

Arabian Sea

Chennai

Bay of Bengal

Yangon

THAILAND

Mindanao
Davao

Bangkok
CAMBODIA

Andaman Is (India)

Phnom Penh

Ho Chi Minh City

BRUNEI

SRI LANKA

Sri Jayewardenepura Kotte

Nicobar Is (India)

MALAYSIA

MALDIVES

Colombo

Kuala Lumpur

Putrajaya

Singapore

Borneo

Celebes

SINGAPORE

Makassar

INDIAN OCEAN

Sumatra

INDONESIA

Dili
EAST TIMOR

Jakarta

Java

Surabaya

Key to symbols

Countries

■ Capital city

○ Important city/town

Other maps showing regions of Asia are on pages:
28-29 Russian Federation
30-31 Southwest and South Asia
32-33 East and Southeast Asia

28-29
30-31
32-33

Shanghai is China's largest city.

A fruit stall in the Chinatown market place, Kuala Lumpur, Malaysia.

The British Isles at the same scale.

AUSTRALIA

0 500 1000 1500 2000 2500 km

Scale : One centimetre on this map is the same as 500 kilometres on the ground.

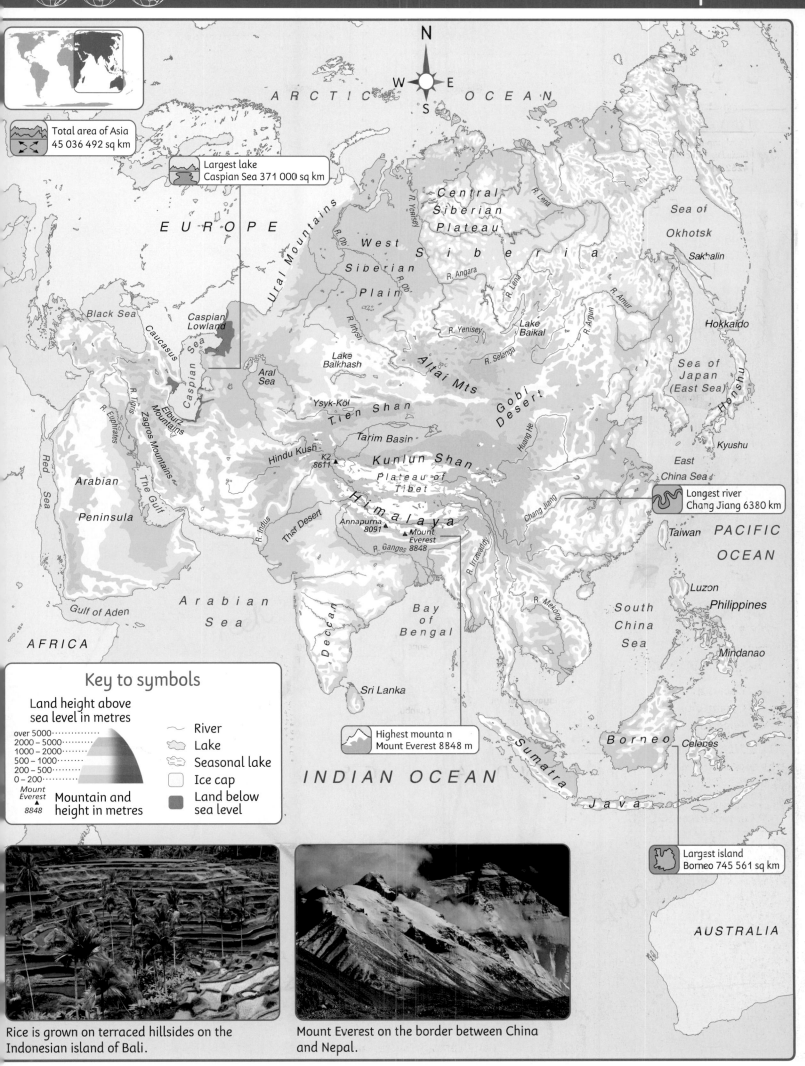

Total area of Asia
45 036 492 sq km

Largest lake
Caspian Sea 371 000 sq km

ARCTIC OCEAN

EUROPE

Black Sea

Caspian Lowland

Caucasus

Caspian Sea

Aral Sea

Ural Mountains

R. Ob

West Siberian Plain

R. Irtysh

Lake Balkhash

Ysyk-Köl

Tien Shan

Tarim Basin

Hindu Kush

K2 8611

Kunlun Shan

Plateau of Tibet

Himalaya

Annapurna 8091

Mount Everest 8848

R. Ganges

Central Siberian Plateau

R. Yenisey

Siberia

R. Angara

R. Yenisey

R. Lena

Lake Baikal

R. Selenga

Altai Mts

Gobi Desert

R. Lena

R. Amur

R. Argun

Sea of Okhotsk

Sakhalin

Hokkaido

Sea of Japan (East Sea)

Honshu

Kyushu

East China Sea

Huang He

Chang Jiang

Longest river
Chang Jiang 6380 km

Taiwan

PACIFIC OCEAN

R. Tigris

R. Euphrates

Elburz Mountains

Zagros Mountains

Red Sea

Arabian Peninsula

The Gulf

R. Indus

Thar Desert

Deccan

R. Irrawaddy

R. Mekong

Luzon

Philippines

South China Sea

Mindanao

Gulf of Aden

Arabian Sea

AFRICA

Bay of Bengal

Sri Lanka

INDIAN OCEAN

Highest mountain
Mount Everest 8848 m

Borneo

Celebes

Sumatra

Java

Largest island
Borneo 745 561 sq km

AUSTRALIA

Key to symbols

Land height above sea level in metres

over 5000
2000 – 5000
1000 – 2000
500 – 1000
200 – 500
0 – 200

Mount Everest 8848 — Mountain and height in metres

- ~ River
- Lake
- Seasonal lake
- Ice cap
- Land below sea level

Rice is grown on terraced hillsides on the Indonesian island of Bali.

Mount Everest on the border between China and Nepal.

500 1000 1500 2000 2500 km

Scale : One centimetre on this map is the same as 500 kilometres on the ground.

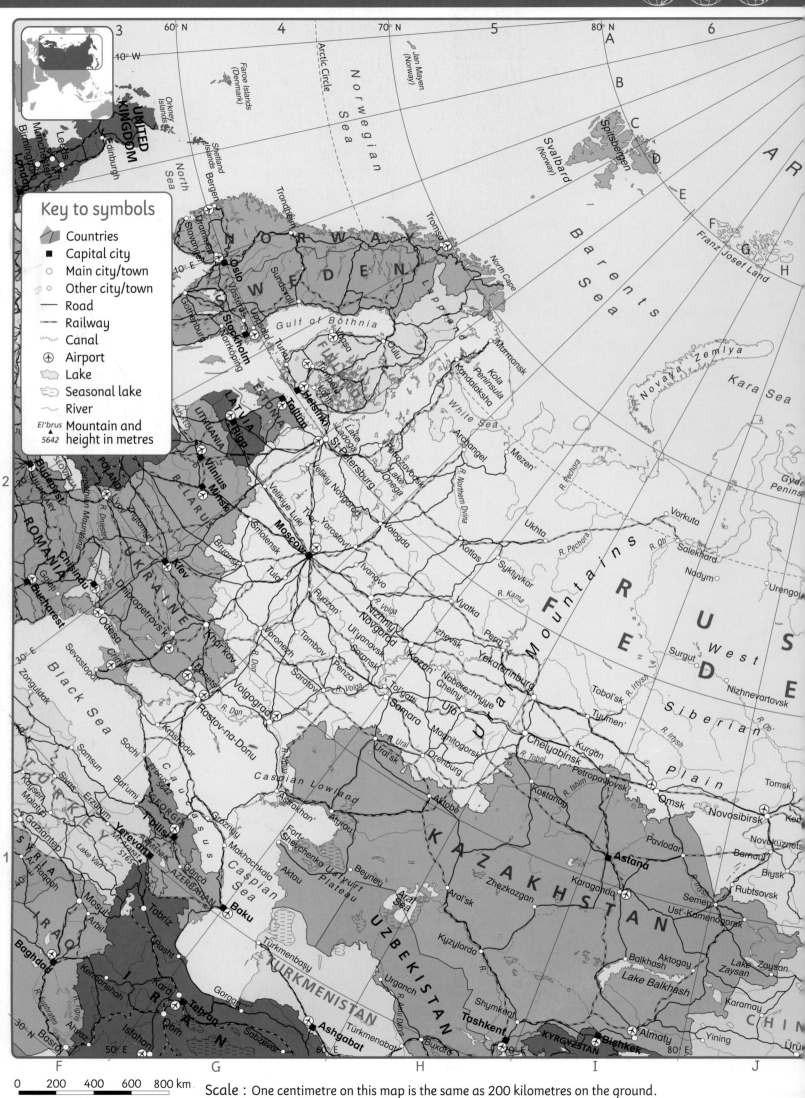

Scale : One centimetre on this map is the same as 200 kilometres on the ground.

Key to symbols

- Countries
- Capital city
- ○ Main city/town
- ○ Other city/town
- —— Road
- ——— Railway
- Canal
- ✈ Airport
- Lake
- Seasonal lake
- River
- ▲ El'brus 5642 Mountain and height in metres

0 200 400 600 800 km

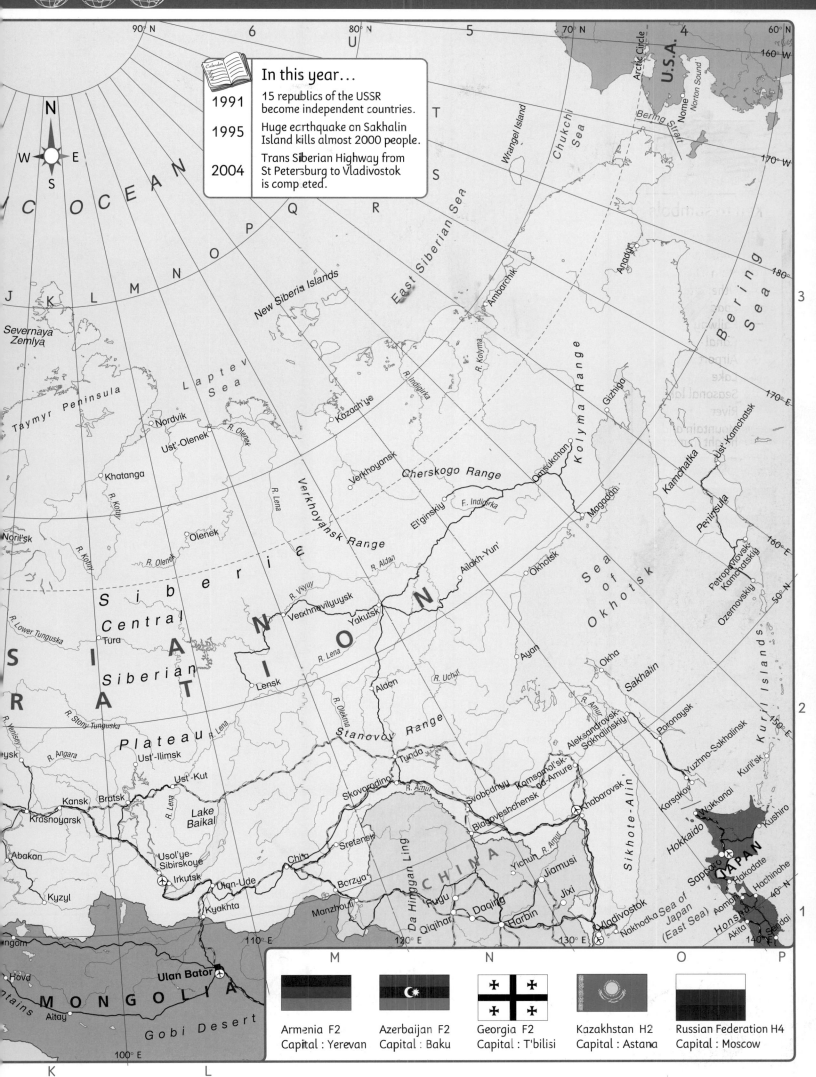

In this year...

1991 15 republics of the USSR become independent countries.

1995 Huge earthquake on Sakhalin Island kills almost 2000 people.

2004 Trans Siberian Highway from St Petersburg to Vladivostok is completed.

ARCTIC OCEAN

U.S.A.

Arctic Circle

RUSSIAN FEDERATION

Severnaya Zemlya

Taymyr Peninsula

New Siberia Islands

Laptev Sea

East Siberian Sea

Chukchi Sea

Wrangel Island

Bering Strait

Nome

Norton Sound

Bering Sea

Kolyma Range

Cherskogo Range

Verkhoyansk Range

Central Siberian Plateau

Siberia

Lake Baikal

Stanovoy Range

Sikhote-Alin'

Kamchatka Peninsula

Sea of Okhotsk

Kuril Islands

Sakhalin

MONGOLIA

CHINA

Da Hinggan Ling

Gobi Desert

JAPAN

Hokkaido

Honshu

Sea of Japan (East Sea)

Nakhodka

Vladivostok

Cities and rivers (labels visible on map):
Noril'sk, Khatanga, Nordvik, Ust'-Olenek, Olenek, R. Olenek, R. Kotuy, R. Lena, Verkhoyansk, Kozach'ye, R. Indigirka, R. Kolyma, Ambarchik, Omsukchan, Gizhiga, Anadyr, Tura, Lensk, Verkhnevilyuysk, Yakutsk, R. Vilyuy, R. Aldan, El'ginskiy, F. Indigirka, Allakh-Yun', Magadan, Ust'-Kamchatsk, Petropavlovsk-Kamchatskiy, Ozernovskiy, R. Lower Tunguska, R. Stony Tunguska, R. Angara, R. Yenisey, Ust'-Ilimsk, Ust'-Kut, Aldan, R. Olekma, Tynda, Okhotsk, Ayan, R. Uchur, Okha, Aleksandrovsk-Sakhalinskiy, Poronaysk, Yuzhno-Sakhalinsk, Kuril'sk, Kansk, Bratsk, R. Lena, Skovorodino, R. Amur, Svobodnyy, Komsomol'sk-na-Amure, Krasnoyarsk, Abakan, Usol'ye-Sibirskoye, Irkutsk, Sretensk, Chita, Blagoveshchensk, Yichun, Jiamusi, Khabarovsk, Korsakov, Kyzyl, Ulan-Ude, Borzya, Hegu, Qiqihar, Daqing, Harbin, Jixi, Nakhodka, Manzhouli, Kyakhta, Ulan Bator, Hovd, Altay, Sapporo, Hakodate, Hachinohe, Akita, Aomori, Sendai

90° N 80° N 70° N 60° N
160° W 170° W 180° 170° E 160° E 150° E 140° E
110° E 120° E 130° E 100° E
60° N 50° N 40° N

Flag	Country	Capital
	Armenia F2	Capital : Yerevan
	Azerbaijan F2	Capital : Baku
	Georgia F2	Capital : T'bilisi
	Kazakhstan H2	Capital : Astana
	Russian Federation H4	Capital : Moscow

N W E S

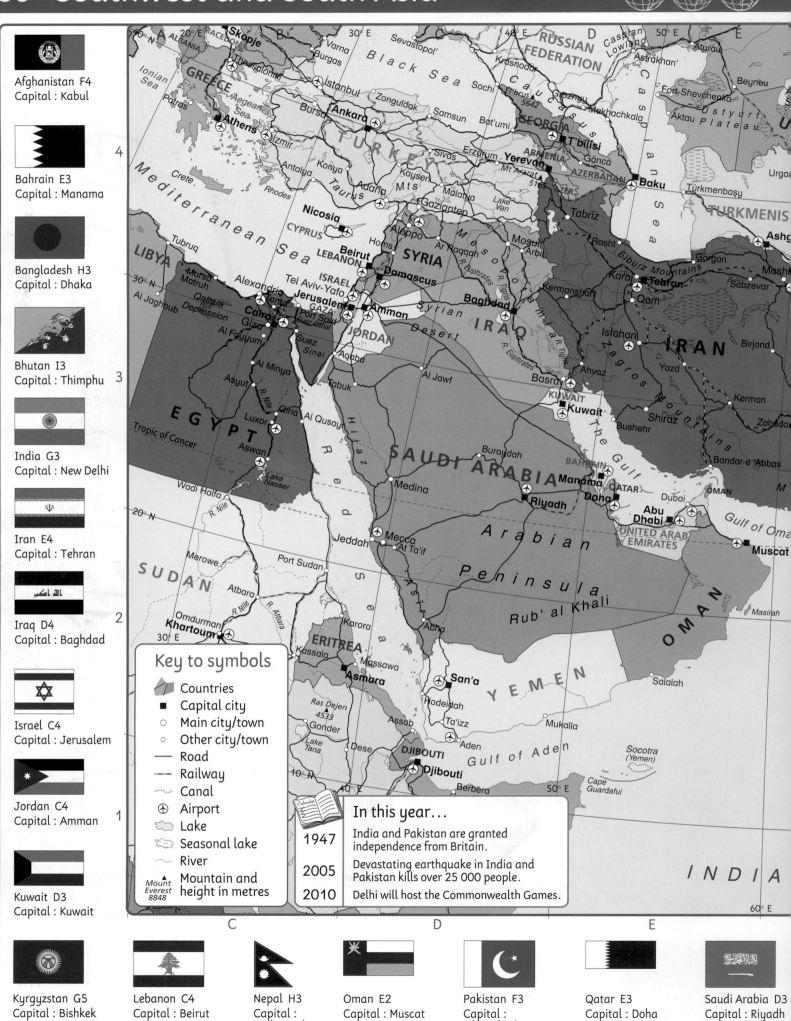

Afghanistan F4
Capital : Kabul

Bahrain E3
Capital : Manama

Bangladesh H3
Capital : Dhaka

Bhutan I3
Capital : Thimphu

India G3
Capital : New Delhi

Iran E4
Capital : Tehran

Iraq D4
Capital : Baghdad

Israel C4
Capital : Jerusalem

Jordan C4
Capital : Amman

Kuwait D3
Capital : Kuwait

Key to symbols

- Countries
- ■ Capital city
- ○ Main city/town
- ∘ Other city/town
- — Road
- — Railway
- Canal
- ✈ Airport
- Lake
- Seasonal lake
- River
- ▲ Mount Everest 8848 Mountain and height in metres

In this year...

1947 India and Pakistan are granted independence from Britain.

2005 Devastating earthquake in India and Pakistan kills over 25 000 people.

2010 Delhi will host the Commonwealth Games.

Kyrgyzstan G5
Capital : Bishkek

Lebanon C4
Capital : Beirut

Nepal H3
Capital : Kathmandu

Oman E2
Capital : Muscat

Pakistan F3
Capital : Islamabad

Qatar E3
Capital : Doha

Saudi Arabia D3
Capital : Riyadh

0   200   400   600   800 km

Scale : One centimetre on this map is the same as 200 kilometres on the ground.

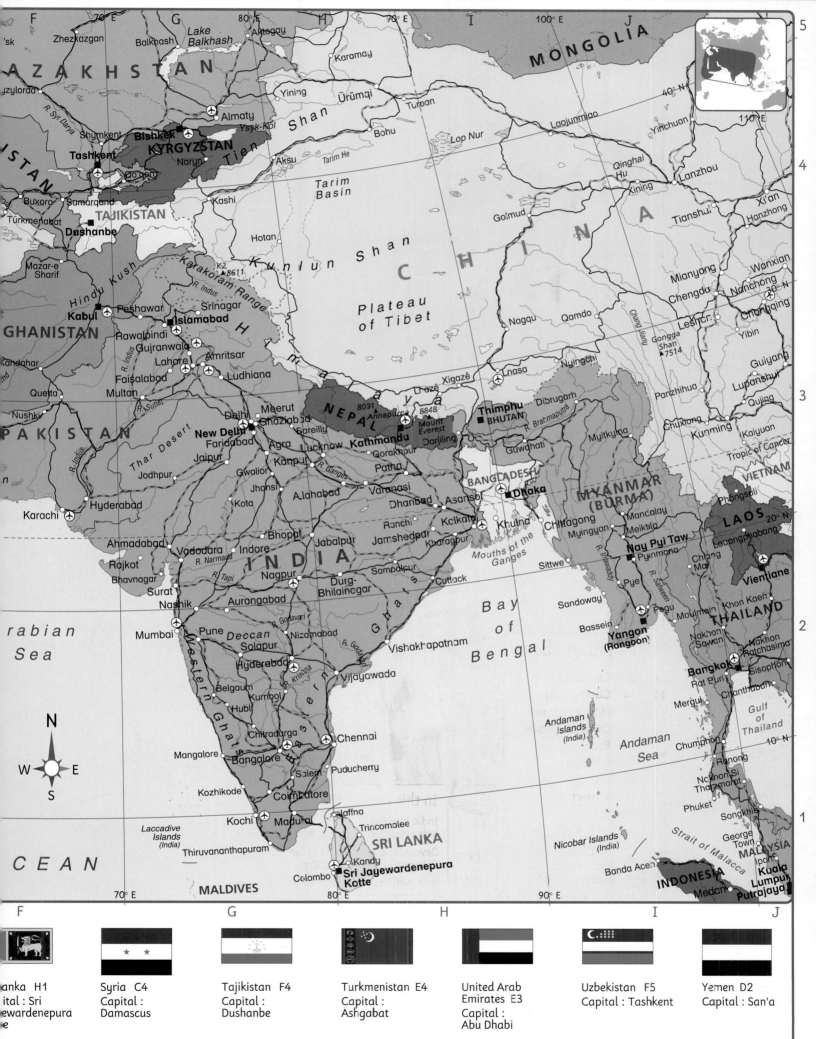

F G H I J

5

4

3

2

1

F G H I J

MONGOLIA

AZAKHSTAN

Zhezkazgan
Balkhash
Lake Balkhash
Aktogay
70° E
80° E
90° E
100° E
40° N
110° E

'sk
Karamay
Yining
Ürümqi
Turpan
Laojunmiao
Yinchuan
Wanxian

Qyzylorda
Almaty
Tien Shan
Bohu
Lop Nur
Qinghai Hu
Lanzhou
Xi'an
30° N

Shymkent
Bishkek
Ysyk-Köl
Aksu
Tarim He
Xining
Tianshui
Hanzhong

Tashkent
KYRGYZSTAN
Naryn
Tarim Basin
Golmud
Mianyang
Nanchong

Buxoro
Samarqand
Qo'qon
Kashi
Hotan
Chengdu
Chongqing

Türkmenabat
TAJIKISTAN
Kunlun Shan
C H I N A
Nagqu
Qamdo
Leshan
Yibin
Guiyang

Dushanbe
K2
8611
Plateau of Tibet
Nyingchi
Chuxiong
Kunming
Kaiyuan

Mazar-e Sharif
Hindu Kush
Karakoram Range
Lhasa
Gongga Shan 7514
Panzhihua
Lupanshui
Qujing

Peshawar
Srinagar
Xigazê
Lhazê
Nyingchi

GHANISTAN
Kabul
Islamabad
Rawalpindi
NEPAL
8031 Annapurna
8848 Mount Everest
Thimphu BHUTAN
Dibrugarh

Kandahar
Gujranwala
Lahore
Amritsar
Ludhiana
Kathmandu
Darjiling
Guwahati
R. Brahmaputra
Myitkyina

Quetta
Faisalabad
Multan
R. Sutlej
Delhi
Ghaziabad
Gorakhpur
Patna
BANGLADESH

PAKISTAN
Nushki
Thar Desert
New Delhi
Faridabad
Bareilly
Lucknow
Dhaka
MYANMAR (BURMA)
Phongsali

R. Indus
Hyderabad
Jaipur
Agra
Kanpur
R. Ganges
Varanasi
Asansol
Khulna
Chittagong
Mandalay
LAOS
20° N

Karachi
Jodhpur
Gwalior
Jhansi
Allahabad
Dhanbad
Ranchi
Kolkata
R. Irrawaddy
Myingyan
Meiktila
Louangphabang

Ahmadabad
Bhopal
Jabalpur
Jamshedpur
Kharagpur
Mouths of the Ganges
Sittwe
Nay Pyi Taw
Pyinmana
Chiang Mai
Vientiane

Rajkot
Vadodara
R. Narmada
INDIA
Nagpur
Durg-Bhilainagar
Samodbar
Cuttack
Pye
Sandoway
THAILAND

Bhavnagar
Surat
Nashik
R. Tapi
Aurangabad
Godavari
Nizamabad
R. Godavari
Vishakhapatnam
Bay of Bengal
Bassein
Yangon (Rangoon)
Pegu
Moulmein
Khon Kaen
Nakhon Ratchasima

Mumbai
Pune
Deccan
Solapur
Hyderabad
R. Krishna
Vijayawada
Ratchaburi
Bangkok
Sisophon

rabian Sea
Belgaum
Kurnool
Western Ghats
Eastern Ghats
Andaman Islands (India)
Mergui
Chanthaburi

Hubli
Chitradurga
Andaman Sea
Gulf of Thailand

Mangalore
Bangalore
Chennai
Chumphon
Ranong

Kozhikode
Coimbatore
Salem
Puducherry
Nakhon Si Thammarat

Kochi
Madurai
Jaffna
Trincomalee
Phuket
Songkhla
George Town
MALAYSIA

Laccadive Islands (India)
SRI LANKA
Nicobar Islands (India)
Strait of Malacca
Ipoh
Kuala Lumpur

CEAN
Thiruvananthapuram
Colombo
Kandy
Sri Jayewardenepura Kotte
Banda Aceh
INDONESIA
Medan
Putrajaya

MALDIVES
70° E
80° E
90° E

Tropic of Cancer
VIETNAM
10° N

N
W E
S

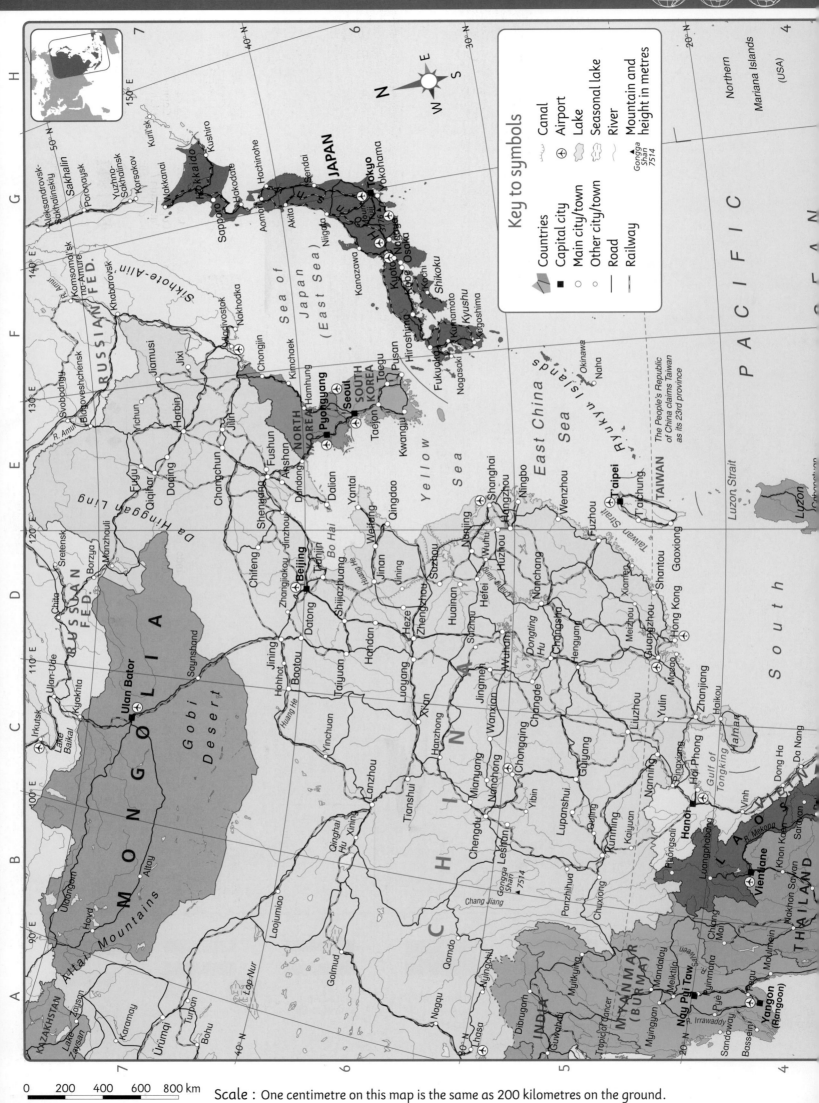

Key to symbols

Countries	Canal
Capital city ■	Airport ⊕
Main city/town ○	Lake
Other city/town ○	Seasonal lake
Road	River
Railway	Mountain and height in metres
	Gongga Shan 7514 ▲

Scale : One centimetre on this map is the same as 200 kilometres on the ground.

0 200 400 600 800 km

The People's Republic of China claims Taiwan as its 23rd province

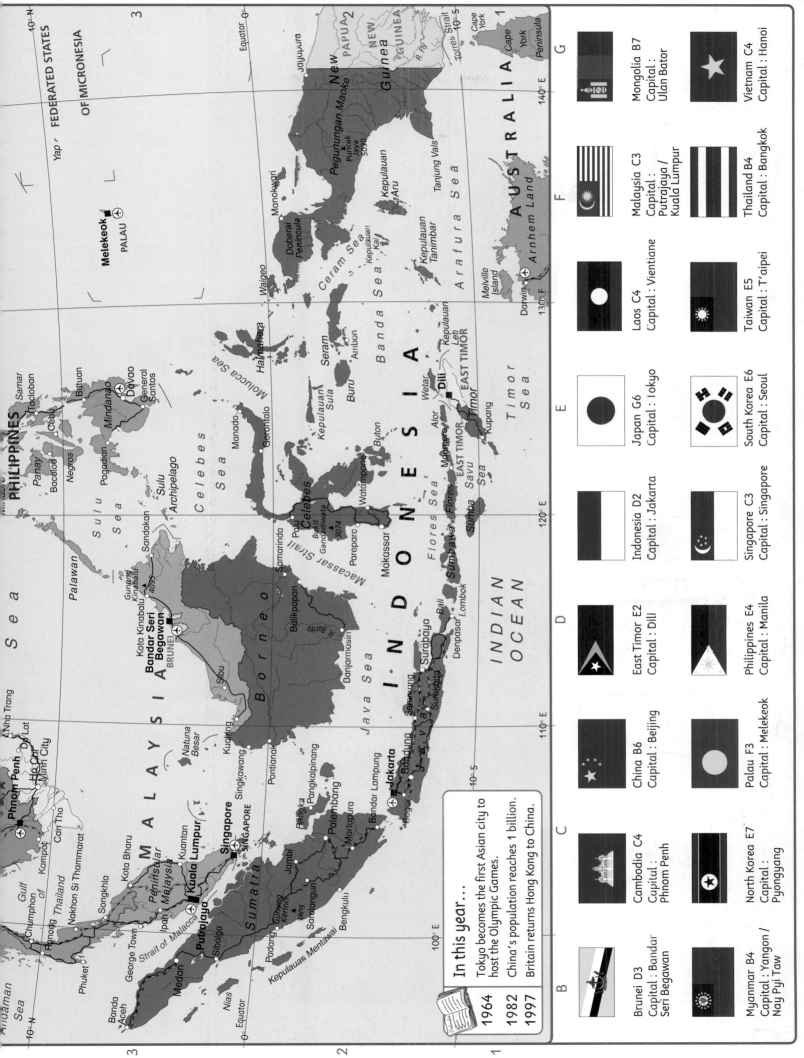

In this year...

1964	Tokyo becomes the first Asian city to host the Olympic Games.
1982	China's population reaches 1 billion.
1997	Britain returns Hong Kong to China.

Brunei D3
Capital : Bandar Seri Begawan

Myanmar B4
Capital : Yangon / Nay Pyi Taw

Cambodia C4
Capital : Phnom Penh

North Korea E7
Capital : Pyongyang

China B6
Capital : Beijing

Palau F3
Capital : Melekeok

East Timor E2
Capital : Dili

Philippines E4
Capital : Manila

Indonesia D2
Capital : Jakarta

Singapore C3
Capital : Singapore

Japan G6
Capital : Tokyo

South Korea E6
Capital : Seoul

Laos C4
Capital : Vientiane

Taiwan E5
Capital : T'aipei

Mongolia B7
Capital : Ulan Bator

Vietnam C4
Capital : Hanoi

Malaysia C3
Capital : Putrajaya / Kuala Lumpur

Thailand B4
Capital : Bangkok

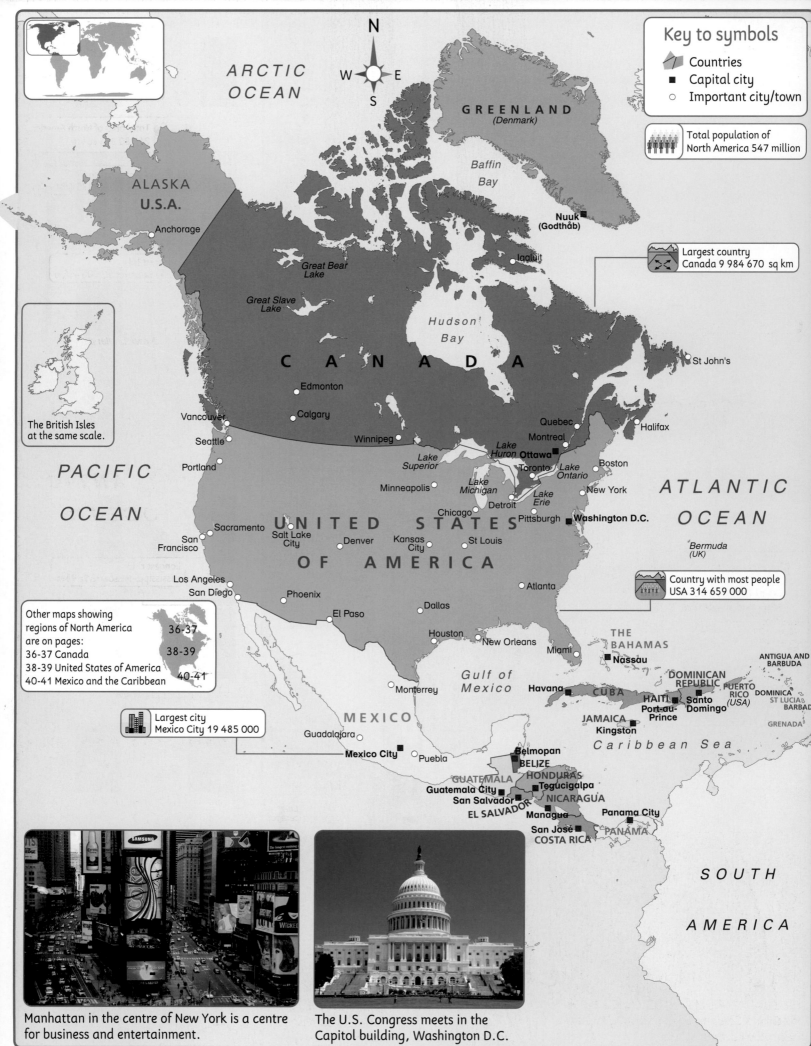

ARCTIC OCEAN

N
W · E
S

GREENLAND
(Denmark)

Baffin Bay

ALASKA
U.S.A.

Anchorage

Key to symbols

Countries
■ Capital city
○ Important city/town

Total population of
North America 547 million

Nuuk
(Godthåb)

Iqaluit

Largest country
Canada 9 984 670 sq km

Great Bear Lake

Great Slave Lake

Hudson Bay

St John's

C A N A D A

Edmonton

The British Isles
at the same scale.

Vancouver

Calgary

Quebec
Montreal

Halifax

Seattle

Winnipeg

Lake Huron Ottawa ■

Boston

PACIFIC OCEAN

Portland

Lake Superior

Toronto Lake Ontario

New York

ATLANTIC OCEAN

Minneapolis

Lake Michigan

Detroit Lake Erie

Chicago

Pittsburgh

Washington D.C.

Sacramento

U N I T E D   S T A T E S

Salt Lake City

Denver

Kansas City

St Louis

Bermuda
(UK)

San Francisco

O F   A M E R I C A

Los Angeles

San Diego

Phoenix

El Paso

Atlanta

Country with most people
USA 314 659 000

Other maps showing
regions of North America
are on pages:
36-37 Canada
38-39 United States of America
40-41 Mexico and the Caribbean

36-37

38-39

40-41

Dallas

Houston

New Orleans

Miami

THE BAHAMAS

Nassau ■

ANTIGUA AND BARBUDA

Monterrey

Gulf of Mexico

Havana ■

CUBA

DOMINICAN REPUBLIC

PUERTO RICO
(USA)

DOMINICA

HAITI
Port-au-Prince

Santo Domingo

ST LUCIA
BARBAD

Largest city
Mexico City 19 485 000

Guadalajara

M E X I C O

JAMAICA
Kingston

GRENADA

Caribbean Sea

Mexico City ■

Puebla

Belmopan ■
BELIZE

GUATEMALA HONDURAS

Panama City ■

Guatemala City ■

Tegucigalpa ■

NICARAGUA

San Salvador ■

EL SALVADOR Managua ■

PANAMA

San José ■
COSTA RICA

SOUTH AMERICA

Manhattan in the centre of New York is a centre
for business and entertainment.

The U.S. Congress meets in the
Capitol building, Washington D.C.

0   400   800   1200   1600 2000 km

Scale : One centimetre on this map is the same as 400 kilometres on the ground.

ASIA

ARCTIC
OCEAN

Greenland

Iceland

Baffin
Bay

Ellesmere Island

Victoria
Island

Davis Strait

Cape Farewell

Total area of North America
24 680 331 sq km

Largest island
Greenland 2 175 600 sq km

R. Yukon

▲ Mount McKinley
6194

Gulf of
Alaska

▲ Mount Logan
5959

Great Bear
Lake

Great Slave
Lake

Baffin Island

Labrador

Newfoundland

Largest lake
Lake Superior 82 100 sq km

R. Mackenzie

Coast Mountains

PACIFIC
OCEAN

R. Peace

3954 ▲

Hudson
Bay

Canadian Shield

Rocky Mountains

Great Plains

Lake Superior

Great
Lakes

Lake Huron

Lake Ontario

R. St. Lawrence

Cape Cod

ATLANTIC
OCEAN

Highest mountain
Mount McKinley 6194 m

R. Snake

Great Salt
Lake

Great
Basin

R. Missouri

Lake
Michigan

Niagara Falls

Lake Erie

R. North Platte

Mount
Elbert
4398

Appalachian Mountains

R. Ohio

▲ 2037

Mount Whitney
4418 ▲

Grand
Canyon

R. Colorado

R. Mississippi

R. Red

Longest river
Mississippi-Missouri 5969 km

Gulf of California

Sierra Madre Occidental

Sierra Madre Oriental

R. Brazos

Rio Grande

Florida

Key to symbols

Land height above sea level in metres

over 5000
2000 – 5000
1000 – 2000
500 – 1000
200 – 500
0 – 200

Mount
McKinley
6194

▲ Mountain and height in metres

〰 River

Lake

Seasonal lake

Polar ice cap

Gulf of
Mexico

Cuba

Hispaniola

Yucatán

Caribbean Sea

Popocatepetl 5452 ▲

Lake
Nicaragua

Isthmus of Panama

SOUTH

AMERICA

The Grand Canyon, a wide, deep gorge in
the southwest of the USA.

The Niagara Falls, a set of massive waterfalls
in Canada and the USA.

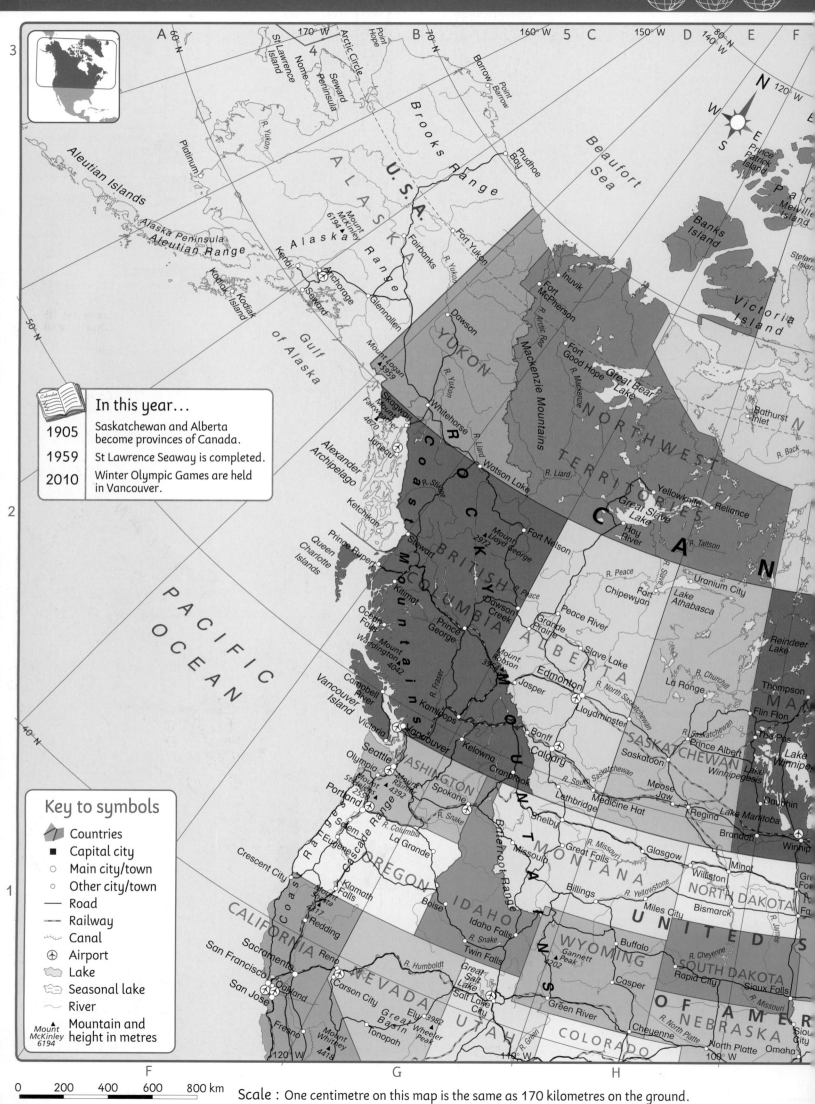

In this year...

1905 Saskatchewan and Alberta become provinces of Canada.

1959 St Lawrence Seaway is completed.

2010 Winter Olympic Games are held in Vancouver.

Key to symbols

- Countries
- ■ Capital city
- ○ Main city/town
- ○ Other city/town
- — Road
- Railway
- Canal
- ⊕ Airport
- Lake
- Seasonal lake
- River
- ▲ *Mount McKinley 6194* Mountain and height in metres

0 200 400 600 800 km

Scale : One centimetre on this map is the same as 170 kilometres on the ground.

Greenland N5
Capital : Nuuk

Canada G4
Capital : Ottawa

CO.	CONNECTICUT
MASS.	MASSACHUSETTS
N.H.	NEW HAMPSHIRE
P.E.I.	PRINCE EDWARD ISLAND
PENN.	PENNSYLVANIA
R.I.	RHODE ISLAND
VER.	VERMONT

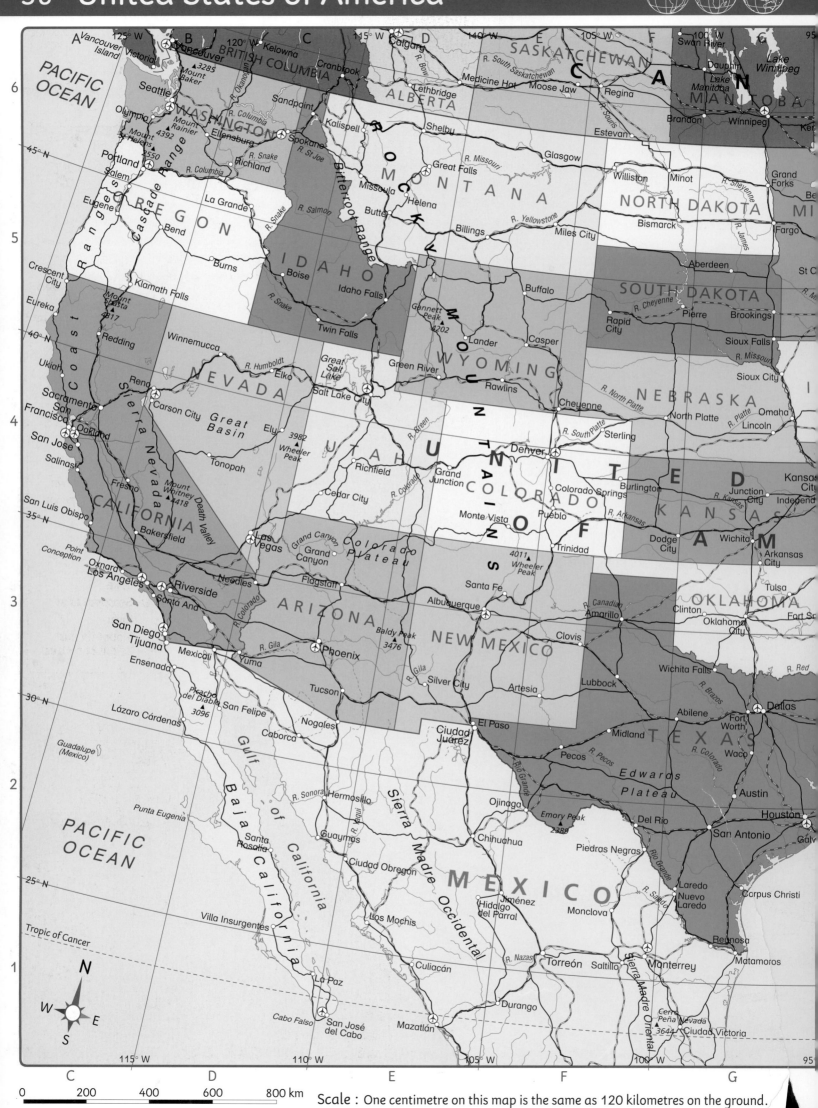

PACIFIC OCEAN

CANADA

125° W · 120° W · 115° W · 110° W · 105° W · 100° W · 95°

Vancouver Island
Victoria
Vancouver
BRITISH COLUMBIA
Kelowna
Cranbrook
Calgary
ALBERTA
SASKATCHEWAN
Swan River
Dauphin
Lake Winnipeg
Lake Manitoba
MANITOBA
Winnipeg
Brandon
Medicine Hat
Moose Jaw
Regina
Estevan
Lethbridge
Shelby

▲ 3285
Mount Baker
Seattle
WASHINGTON
Olympia
Mount Rainier 4392
Mount St. Helens 3550
Sandpoint
R. Okanogan
R. Columbia
Spokane
Ellensburg
Richland
R. Snake
R. St Joe
Kalispell
Missoula
Helena
Great Falls
R. Missouri
Glasgow
MONTANA
Williston
Minot
R. Cheyenne
Grand Forks
NORTH DAKOTA
Bismarck
R. James
Fargo
MI

45° N

Portland
Salem
Eugene
OREGON
Cascade Range
Coast Ranges
La Grande
R. Columbia
R. Snake
Bend
Burns
IDAHO
Boise
Bitterroot Range
R. Salmon
R. Snake
Butte
Billings
R. Yellowstone
Miles City
ROCKY
MONTANA
Buffalo
Rapid City
SOUTH DAKOTA
Pierre
Brookings
Aberdeen

40° N

Crescent City
Eureka
Ukiah
Redding
Mount Shasta ▲ 4317
Klamath Falls
Winnemucca
R. Humboldt
Elko
Idaho Falls
Twin Falls
Gannett Peak ▲ 4202
Lander
WYOMING
Green River
Casper
MOUNTAINS
Sioux Falls
R. Missouri
Sioux City
NEBRASKA
I

35° N

San Francisco
Sacramento
San Jose
Oakland
Salinas
Reno
Carson City
Sierra Nevada
NEVADA
Great Basin
Ely
3982 Wheeler Peak
Tonopah
Great Salt Lake
Salt Lake City
UTAH
R. Green
Rawlins
Richfield
Grand Junction
R. Colorado
Denver
UNITED
Cheyenne
Sterling
R. North Platte
North Platte
R. Platte
Lincoln
Omaha
Burlington
Junction City
Independence
Kansas City
D

San Luis Obispo
Point Conception
CALIFORNIA
Fresno
Bakersfield
Mount Whitney ▲ 4418
Death Valley
Las Vegas
Needles
R. Colorado
Grand Canyon
Grand Canyon
Cedar City
Colorado Plateau
Flagstaff
COLORADO
Monte Vista
Pueblo
Colorado Springs
Santa Fe
4011 ▲ Wheeler Peak
R. Arkansas
Trinidad
STATES
OF
KANSAS
Dodge City
Wichita
AM
Arkansas City

Los Angeles
Oxnard
Riverside
Santa Ana
San Diego
Tijuana
Mexicali
Ensenada
R. Gila
Yuma
ARIZONA
Phoenix
Baldy Peak ▲ 3476
Tucson
R. Gila
Silver City
NEW MEXICO
Albuquerque
Amarillo
R. Canadian
Clovis
Clinton
OKLAHOMA
Oklahoma City
Fort Sm
Tulsa
R. Red

30° N

Picacho del Diablo ▲ 3096
San Felipe
Nogales
Caborca
Lázaro Cárdenas
Mexicali
El Paso
Ciudad Juárez
Artesia
Lubbock
Midland
TEXAS
Pecos
R. Pecos
Abilene
Wichita Falls
Fort Worth
Dallas
Waco
R. Colorado
R. Brazos

Guadalupe (Mexico)
Punta Eugenia
Ensenada
Baja California
Gulf of California
R. Sonora
Hermosillo
R. Yaqui
Guaymas
Sierra Madre Occidental
Chihuahua
Ojinaga
Emory Peak ▲ 2388
Del Rio
Edwards Plateau
Austin
San Antonio
Houston
Gal

25° N

PACIFIC OCEAN
Santa Rosalía
Villa Insurgentes
La Paz
Ciudad Obregón
Los Mochis
MEXICO
Hidalgo del Parral
Jiménez
Chihuahua
Piedras Negras
Monclova
Rio Grande
R. Salado
Laredo
Nuevo Laredo
Corpus Christi
Reynosa
Matamoros

Tropic of Cancer

Cabo Falso
San José del Cabo
Mazatlán
Culiacán
Durango
R. Nazas
Torreón
Saltillo
Monterrey
Cerro Peña Nevada ▲ 3644
Ciudad Victoria
Sierra Madre Oriental

N
W E
S

115° W · 110° W · 105° W · 100° W · 95°

0   200   400   600   800 km

Scale : One centimetre on this map is the same as 120 kilometres on the ground.

Key to symbols

- ◥ Countries
- ■ Capital city
- ○ Main city/town
- ○ Other city/town
- — Road
- — Railway
- ⌇ Canal
- ⊕ Airport
- Lake
- Seasonal lake
- River
- ▲ Mountain and
  Mount Whitney 4418 height in metres

CO.   CONNECTICUT
MASS. MASSACHUSETTS
N.H. NEW HAMPSHIRE
P.E.I. PRINCE EDWARD ISLAND
R.I. RHODE ISLAND
VER. VERMONT

United States of
America D4
Capital : Washington D.C.

In this year...

1886	Statue of Liberty is erected on Liberty Island, New York.
2001	The September 11 attacks destroy the World Trade Center in New York City.
2005	Hurricane Katrina devastates New Orleans and parts of the Gulf Coast.
2009	Barack Obama becomes the USA's first black president.

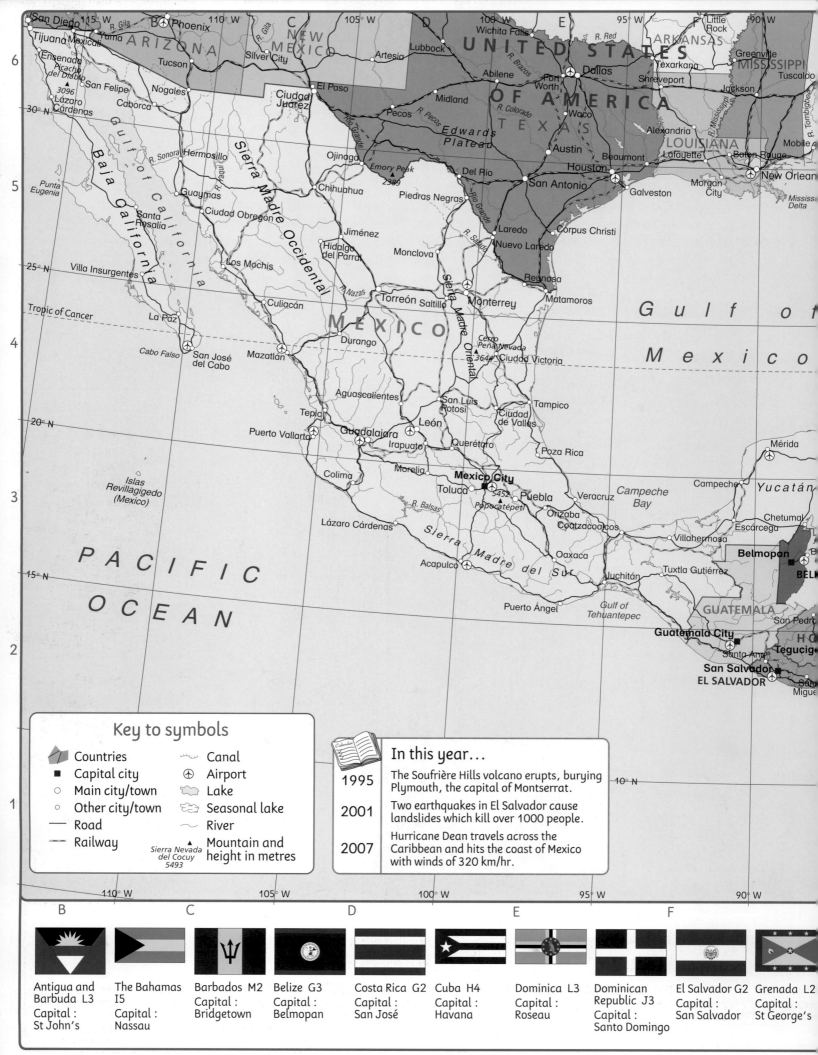

Key to symbols

Symbol	Meaning	Symbol	Meaning
◤	Countries	∿	Canal
■	Capital city	⊕	Airport
○	Main city/town	◠	Lake
○	Other city/town	◠	Seasonal lake
—	Road	∼	River
▦	Railway	▲	Mountain and
	Sierra Nevada del Cocuy 5493		height in metres

In this year...

1995	The Soufrière Hills volcano erupts, burying Plymouth, the capital of Montserrat.
2001	Two earthquakes in El Salvador cause landslides which kill over 1000 people.
2007	Hurricane Dean travels across the Caribbean and hits the coast of Mexico with winds of 320 km/hr.

Antigua and Barbuda L3
Capital : St John's

The Bahamas I5
Capital : Nassau

Barbados M2
Capital : Bridgetown

Belize G3
Capital : Belmopan

Costa Rica G2
Capital : San José

Cuba H4
Capital : Havana

Dominica L3
Capital : Roseau

Dominican Republic J3
Capital : Santo Domingo

El Salvador G2
Capital : San Salvador

Grenada L2
Capital : St George's

0 200 400 600 800 km

Scale : One centimetre on this map is the same as 135 kilometres on the ground.

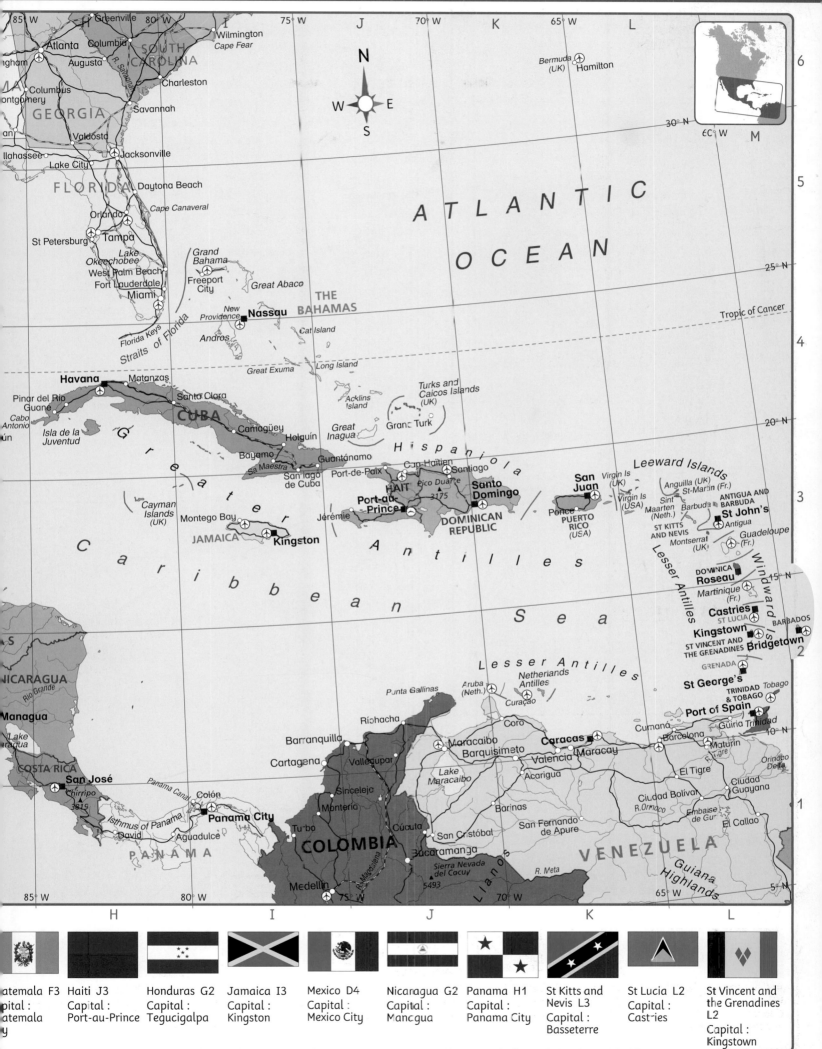

NORTH AMERICA

Caribbean Sea

Key to symbols
- ◢ Countries
- ■ Capital city
- ○ Important city/town

Total population of South America
393 million

ATLANTIC OCEAN

Barranquilla
Maracaibo
Caracas ■
Port of Spain ■
TRINIDAD AND TOBAGO

VENEZUELA

Medellín

Georgetown ■
Paramaribo ■
GUYANA
SURINAME
Cayenne ■
FRENCH GUIANA

■ Bogotá
COLOMBIA

Cali

Quito ■
ECUADOR

Largest country
Brazil 8 514 879 sq km

Country with most people
Brazil 193 734 000

Galapagos Islands
(Ecuador)

Guayaquil

Belém

São Luís

Iquitos

Manaus ○

Fortaleza

Natal

Trujillo

B R A Z I L

PERU

Recife

Lima ■

Aracaju

PACIFIC

Salvador

OCEAN

Lake Titicaca

BOLIVIA

La Paz ■

Arequipa

Sucre ■

Brasília ■

Largest city
São Paulo 19 582 000

Belo Horizonte

Antofagasta

PARAGUAY

Rio de Janeiro

São Paulo ○

Asunción ■

The British Isles
at the same scale.

Valparaíso

Curitiba

C
H
I
L
E

ATLANTIC

Porto Alegre

OCEAN

Other maps showing regions
of South America are on pages: 44-45
44-45 South America

Santiago ■

A
R
G
E
N
T
I
N
A

URUGUAY

Buenos Aires ■

Montevideo ■

Concepción

Mar del Plata

Punta Arenas

Tierra del Fuego

Falkland Islands
(UK)

South Georgia
(UK)

South Orkney
Islands
(UK)

Antarctic
Peninsula

The statue known as Christ the Redeemer over-
looks Rio de Janeiro.

The ruins of the lost Inca city of
Machu Picchu in Peru.

0 400 800 1200 1600 2000 km
Scale : One centimetre on this map is the same as 400 kilometres on the ground.

Key to symbols

Land height above sea level in metres

over 5000
2000 – 5000
1000 – 2000
500 – 1000
200 – 500
0 – 200

Aconcagua
▲
6959 **Mountain and height in metres**

∿ River

⬭ Lake

⬭ Seasonal lake

Total area of South America
17 815 420 sq km

Longest river
River Amazon 6516 km

Largest lake
Lake Titicaca 8340 sq km

Highest mountain
Aconcagua 6959 m

Largest island
Tierra del Fuego 47 000 sq km

Caribbean Sea

ATLANTIC OCEAN

Lake Maracaibo

Orinoco Delta

R. Orinoco

Llanos

Angel Falls

Mount Roraima 2810

Guiana Highlands

Mouths of the Amazon

R. Japurá

R. Negro

R. Amazon

Galapagos Islands

R. Amazon

Amazon Basin

Selvas

R. Madeira

R. Purus

R. Tocantins

R. São Francisco

PACIFIC OCEAN

Andes

Lake Titicaca

Altiplano

Atacama Desert

Brazilian Highlands

Gran Chaco

R. Paraguay

Nevado Ojos del Salado 6908

R. Salado

R. Paraná

R. Paraná

R. Uruguay

ATLANTIC OCEAN

Juan Fernandez Islands

Aconcagua 6959

Pampas

Rio de la Plata

R. Colorado

R. Negro

Valdes Peninsula

Isla de Chiloé

Patagonia

Falkland Islands

Tierra del Fuego

Cape Horn

South Georgia

Antarctic Peninsula

South Orkney Islands

N
W   E
S

Wild horses in Patagonia, Argentina.

The Amazon rain forest covers more than one third of Brazil.

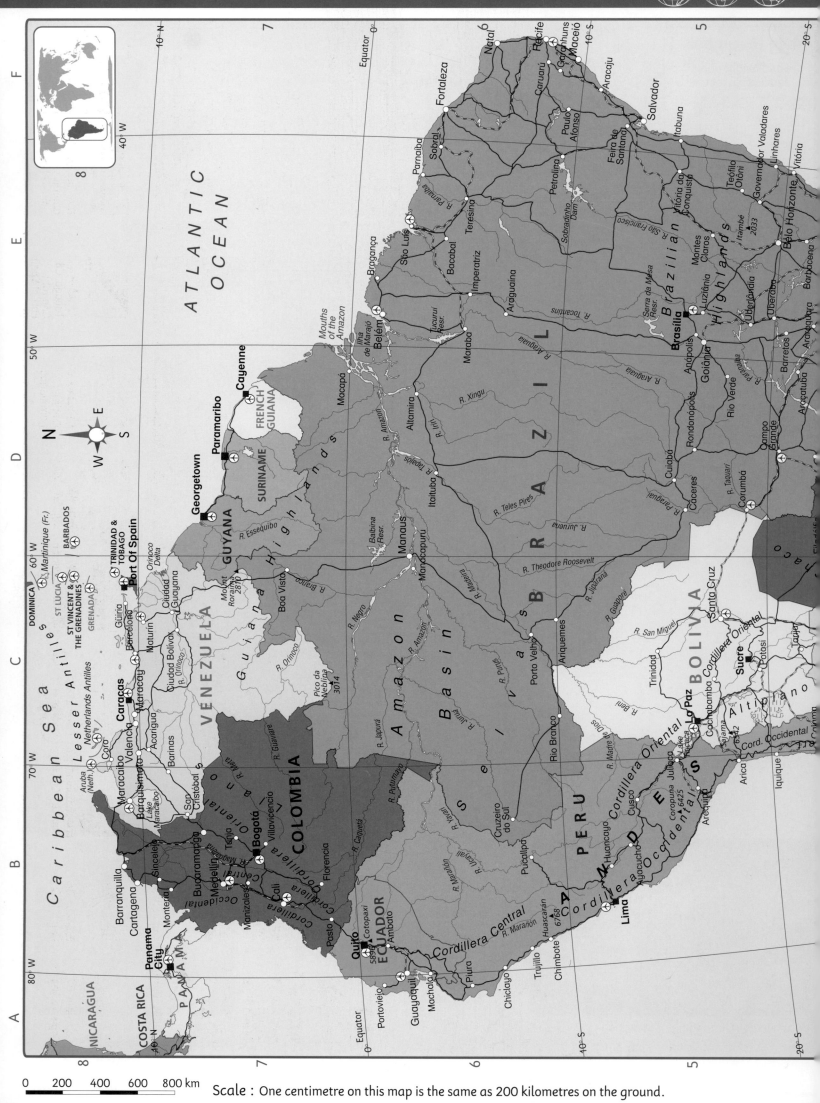

ATLANTIC OCEAN

Caribbean Sea

Lesser Antilles

Netherlands Antilles

Aruba (Neth.)

DOMINICA
ST LUCIA
ST VINCENT &
THE GRENADINES
BARBADOS
GRENADA
Martinique (Fr.)
TRINIDAD & TOBAGO
Port Of Spain

N
W — E
S

VENEZUELA
Caracas
Maracaibo
Valencia
Maracay
Barquisimeto
Coro
Acarigua
Barinas
Maturín
Barcelona
Güiria
Ciudad Bolívar
Ciudad Guayana
Orinoco Delta
R. Orinoco
Pico da Neblina 3014
Mount Roraima 2810

GUYANA
Georgetown
R. Essequibo

SURINAME
Paramaribo

FRENCH GUIANA
Cayenne

Guiana Highlands

Mouths of the Amazon
Ilha de Marajó
Belém
Bragança
São Luís
Macapá
Boa Vista
R. Branco
R. Negro
Manaus
Manacapuru
Altamira
Itaituba
R. Tapajós
R. Xingu
R. Iriri
R. Teles Pires
Balbina Resr.

BRAZIL
Fortaleza
Natal
Recife
Maceió
Garanhuns
Aracaju
Caruaru
Paulo Afonso
Feira de Santana
Salvador
Itabuna
Teresina
Sobral
Parnaíba
R. Parnaíba
Imperatriz
Marabá
Araguaína
Bacabal
R. Tocantins
R. Araguaia
Tucuruí Resr.
Petrolina
Sobradinho Dam
R. São Francisco
Montes Claros
Serra da Mesa Resr.
Brazilian Highlands
Itambé 2033
Teófilo Otoni
Governador Valadares
Linhares
Vitória da Conquista
Belo Horizonte
Vitória
Barbacena
Araçuaí
Araçatuba
Barretos
Campo Grande
Uberaba
Uberlândia
Anápolis
Goiânia
Luziânia
Brasília
Rio Verde
Rondonópolis
Cuiabá
Cáceres
R. Taquari
Corumbá
Chaco
R. Paraguai

COLOMBIA
Bogotá
Medellín
Cali
Manizales
Bucaramanga
Cúcuta
Tunja
Villavicencio
Florencia
San Cristóbal
Montería
Sincelejo
Barranquilla
Cartagena
Lake Maracaibo
Panama City
Llanos Orientales
R. Meta
R. Guaviare
R. Vichada
R. Putumayo
R. Caquetá
R. Magdalena
Cordillera Occidental
Cordillera Central
Cordillera Oriental

ECUADOR
Quito
Guayaquil
Ambato
Cotopaxi 5896
Portoviejo
Machala
Cuenca

PERU
Lima
Trujillo
Chiclayo
Chimbote
Piura
Pucallpa
Cruzeiro do Sul
Cusco
Huancayo
Ayacucho
Arequipa
Huascarán 6768
Cordillera Central
Cordillera Occidental
Cordillera Oriental
R. Marañón
R. Ucayali
R. Huallaga
R. Madre de Dios
Lake Titicaca
Lake Junín

BOLIVIA
La Paz
Sucre
Santa Cruz
Cochabamba
Potosí
Trinidad
Cordillera Oriental
Cordillera Occidental
Altiplano
Coropuna 6425
Coropuna Juliaca
Arica
Iquique
R. San Miguel
R. Guaporé
R. Beni
R. Mamoré

A N D E S

Amazon Basin
Selvas
R. Amazon
R. Amazonas
R. Madeira
R. Purus
R. Juruá
R. Japurá
R. Jiparaná
R. Juruena
R. Theodore Roosevelt
R. Guaporé
Porto Velho
Ariquemes
Rio Branco

NICARAGUA
COSTA RICA
PANAMA

---

0 200 400 600 800 km

Scale : One centimetre on this map is the same as 200 kilometres on the ground.

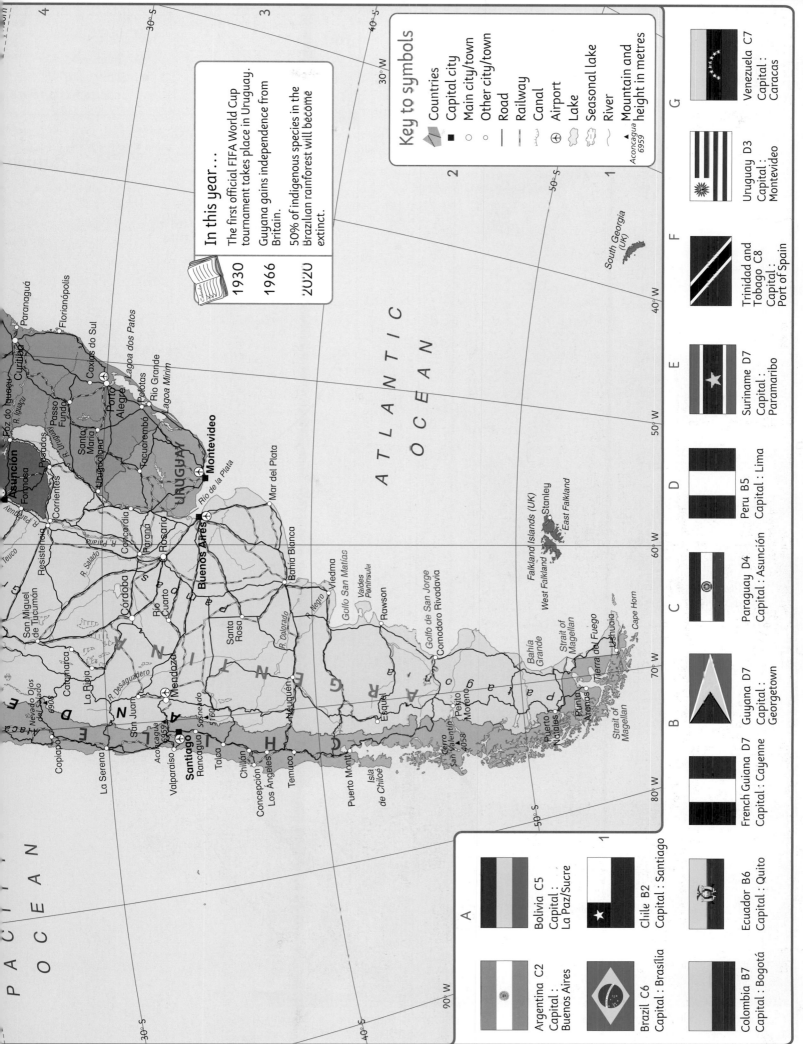

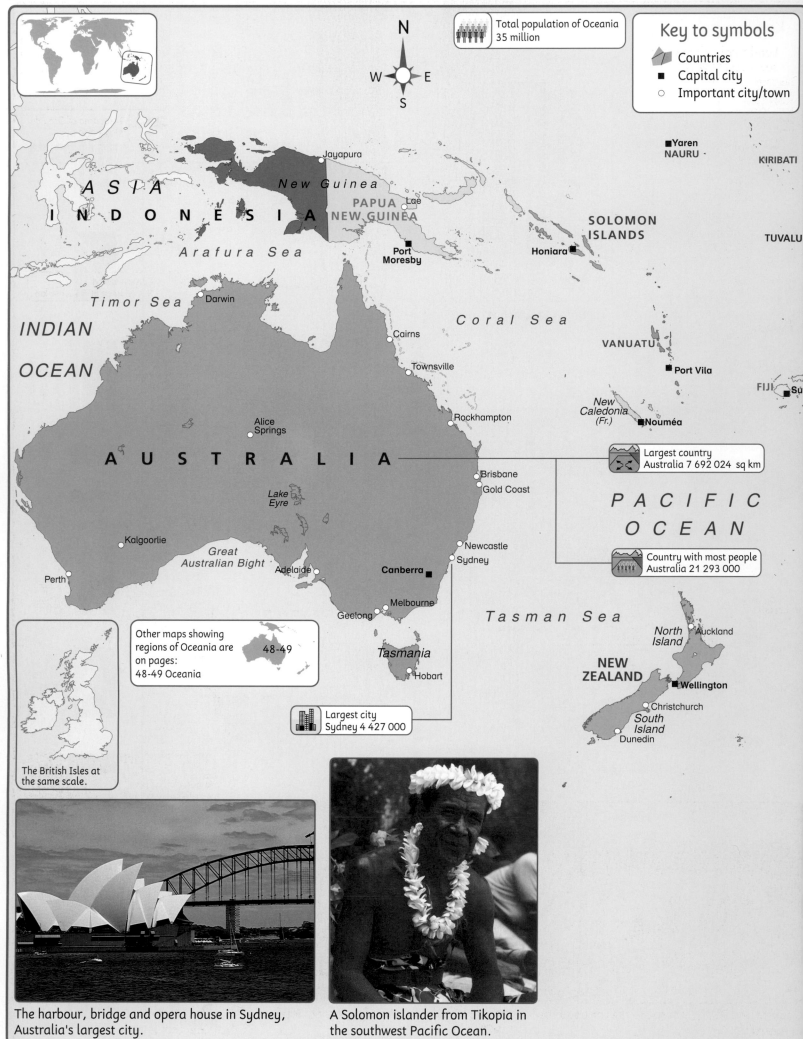

Total population of Oceania
35 million

Key to symbols

◤ Countries
■ Capital city
○ Important city/town

N W E S (compass)

ASIA

INDONESIA

New Guinea

Jayapura

Lae

PAPUA NEW GUINEA

Port Moresby

■Yaren
NAURU

KIRIBATI

SOLOMON ISLANDS

Honiara■

TUVALU

Arafura Sea

Timor Sea

Darwin

Coral Sea

INDIAN OCEAN

Cairns

Townsville

VANUATU

■ Port Vila

FIJI ■Su

Alice Springs

AUSTRALIA

Rockhampton

New Caledonia (Fr.)
■Nouméa

Largest country
Australia 7 692 024 sq km

Lake Eyre

Brisbane
Gold Coast

P A C I F I C

O C E A N

Kalgoorlie

Great Australian Bight

Adelaide

Newcastle
Sydney

Canberra ■

Country with most people
Australia 21 293 000

Perth

Melbourne

Geelong

Tasman Sea

North Island

Auckland

Other maps showing regions of Oceania are on pages:
48-49 Oceania

48-49

Tasmania

Hobart

NEW ZEALAND

■**Wellington**

Christchurch

South Island

Dunedin

Largest city
Sydney 4 427 000

The British Isles at the same scale.

The harbour, bridge and opera house in Sydney, Australia's largest city.

A Solomon islander from Tikopia in the southwest Pacific Ocean.

0 300 600 900 1200 1500 km

Scale : One centimetre on this map is the same as 325 kilometres on the ground.

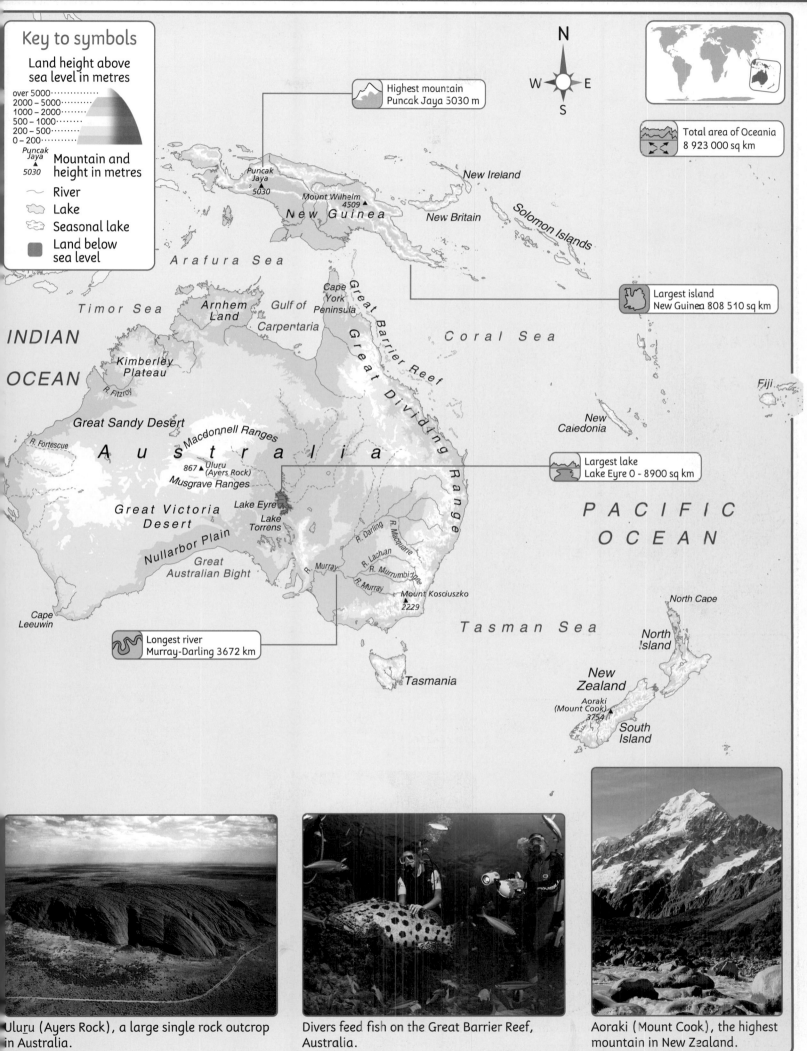

Key to symbols

Land height above sea level in metres

over 5000
2000 – 5000
1000 – 2000
500 – 1000
200 – 500
0 – 200

Puncak Jaya ▲ 5030 Mountain and height in metres

~ River

Lake

Seasonal lake

Land below sea level

Highest mountain
Puncak Jaya 5030 m

Total area of Oceania
8 923 000 sq km

Largest island
New Guinea 808 510 sq km

Largest lake
Lake Eyre 0 - 8900 sq km

Longest river
Murray-Darling 3672 km

Puncak Jaya ▲ 5030

New Guinea

Mount Wilhelm 4509 ▲

New Ireland

New Britain

Solomon Islands

Arafura Sea

Timor Sea

INDIAN OCEAN

Cape York Peninsula

Arnhem Land

Gulf of Carpentaria

Coral Sea

Kimberley Plateau

R. Fitzroy

Great Sandy Desert

R. Fortescue

A u s t r a l i a

Macdonnell Ranges

867 ▲ Uluru (Ayers Rock)

Musgrave Ranges

Great Victoria Desert

Lake Eyre

Lake Torrens

Nullarbor Plain

Great Australian Bight

R. Murray

R. Darling

R. Macquarie

R. Lachlan

R. Murrumbidgee

R. Murray

Great Dividing Range

Great Barrier Reef

New Caledonia

Fiji

PACIFIC OCEAN

Mount Kosciuszko 2229

Tasman Sea

Cape Leeuwin

Tasmania

North Cape

North Island

New Zealand

Aoraki (Mount Cook) 3754

South Island

Uluru (Ayers Rock), a large single rock outcrop in Australia.

Divers feed fish on the Great Barrier Reef, Australia.

Aoraki (Mount Cook), the highest mountain in New Zealand.

300   600   900   1200   1500 km

Scale : One centimetre on this map is the same as 325 kilometres on the ground.

Key to symbols

◤	Countries	⊕	Airport
■	Capital city	🗻	Lake
○	Main city/town	🗻	Seasonal lake
○	Other city/town	～	River
—	Road	▲ Puncak Jaya 5030	Mountain and height in metres
—	Railway		

Scale : One centimetre on this map is the same as 200 kilometres on the ground.

0 200 400 600 800 km

160° E   170° E   180°   170° W

N
W E
S

NAURU

Kingsmill Group

KIRIBATI

Phoenix Islands

SOLOMON ISLANDS

TUVALU

6

Santa Isabel
Malaita

Funafuti
Vaiaku

Tokelau (New Zealand)

10° S

...ara ■
...alcanal   San Cristobal

Wallis and Futuna Islands (France)

SAMOA

American Samoa (USA)

5

VANUATU

Savai'i
Upolu   ■ **Apia**

Espíritu Santo
Malakula

Vanua Levu

Éfaté ■ **Port Vila**

FIJI

Viti Levu   ■ **Suva**

Niue (New Zealand)

New Caledonia (France)

Îles Loyauté

20° S

■ **Nouméa**

Nuku'alofa ■   TONGA

4

Tropic of Capricorn

P A C I F I C   O C E A N

30° S

North Cape

North Island

Auckland

2002 — A powerful earthquake causes major damage to Vanuatu's capital, Port Vila.

In this year…

Manukau
Hamilton

2006 — North Queensland is declared a natural disaster zone as severe tropical cyclone Larry hits the coast.

Mount Taranaki (Mount Egmont) ▲ 2518

Palmerston North   Napier

2007 — Sydney Opera House is listed as a World Heritage Site.

Sea

NEW ZEALAND

Nelson   ■ **Wellington**

3

Aoraki (Mount Cook)
▲ 3754

South Island   Southern Alps   Christchurch

Chatham Islands (New Zealand)

40° S

Cape Providence   Lake Te Anau

Dunedin

Auckland Islands (New Zealand)

170° E   50° S   180°   170° W   160° W

F   G   H   I   J

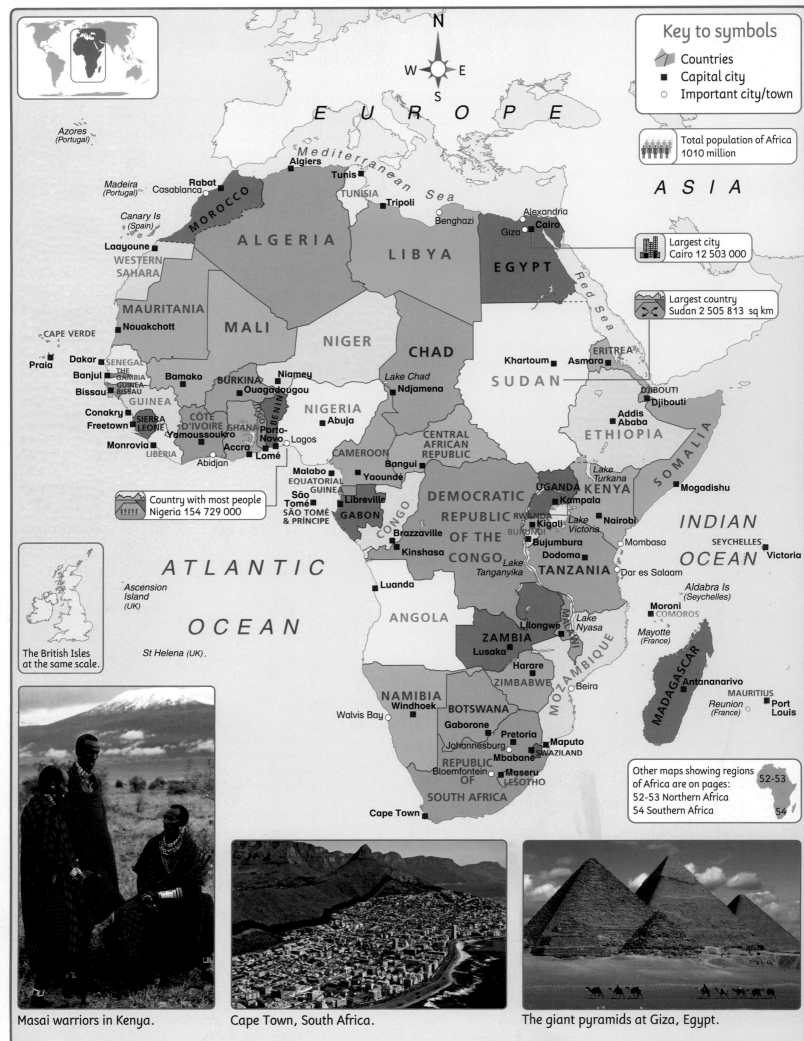

Azores
(Portugal)

EUROPE

Mediterranean Sea

Key to symbols

- Countries
- ■ Capital city
- ○ Important city/town

Total population of Africa
1010 million

ASIA

Algiers
Tunis
TUNISIA
Tripoli
Benghazi
Alexandria
Cairo
Giza

Largest city
Cairo 12 503 000

Madeira
(Portugal)
Casablanca
Rabat
MOROCCO

Canary Is
(Spain)
Laayoune
WESTERN
SAHARA

ALGERIA

LIBYA

EGYPT

Red Sea

Largest country
Sudan 2 505 813 sq km

MAURITANIA
Nouakchott

MALI

NIGER

CHAD

Lake Chad
Ndjamena

Khartoum
SUDAN
Asmara
ERITREA

DJIBOUTI
Djibouti

CAPE VERDE

Praia

Dakar
SENEGAL
THE
Banjul GAMBIA
Bissau GUINEA-
BISSAU
Conakry
Freetown
SIERRA
LEONE
Monrovia
LIBERIA

Bamako
BURKINA
Ouagadougou

Niamey

NIGERIA
Abuja

CÔTE
D'IVOIRE
Yamoussoukro
GHANA
Accra
Abidjan
Lomé
BENIN
TOGO
Porto-
Novo
Lagos

CAMEROON
Bangui

CENTRAL
AFRICAN
REPUBLIC

Addis
Ababa
ETHIOPIA

SOMALIA

Mogadishu

Country with most people
Nigeria 154 729 000

Malabo
EQUATORIAL
GUINEA
São
Tomé
SÃO TOMÉ
& PRÍNCIPE
GABON
Libreville
CONGO
Brazzaville
Kinshasa

Yaoundé

DEMOCRATIC
REPUBLIC
OF THE
CONGO

UGANDA
Kampala
RWANDA
Kigali
BURUNDI
Bujumbura
Lake
Victoria
Lake
Tanganyika
TANZANIA
Dodoma

KENYA
Nairobi
Lake
Turkana

Mombasa

INDIAN
OCEAN

SEYCHELLES
Victoria

Dar es Salaam

Aldabra Is
(Seychelles)

ATLANTIC

Ascension
Island
(UK)

OCEAN

St Helena (UK)

The British Isles
at the same scale.

Luanda

ANGOLA

Lilongwe
MALAWI
Lake
Nyasa
ZAMBIA
Lusaka
Harare
ZIMBABWE
Beira

Moroni
COMOROS

Mayotte
(France)

MADAGASCAR
Antananarivo
MAURITIUS
Reunion
(France)
Port
Louis

MOZAMBIQUE

NAMIBIA
Windhoek
Walvis Bay

BOTSWANA
Gaborone
Johannesburg
Pretoria
Mbabane
SWAZILAND
Maputo

Other maps showing regions
of Africa are on pages:
52-53 Northern Africa
54 Southern Africa

52-53

54

REPUBLIC
OF
SOUTH AFRICA
Bloemfontein
Maseru
LESOTHO

Cape Town

Masai warriors in Kenya.

Cape Town, South Africa.

The giant pyramids at Giza, Egypt.

Key to symbols

Land height above sea level in metres
- over 5000
- 2000 – 5000
- 1000 – 2000
- 500 – 1000
- 200 – 500
- 0 – 200

Kilimanjaro 5892 ▲ Mountain and height in metres

River

Lake

Land below sea level

Longest river River Nile 6695 km

Total area of Africa 30 343 578 sq km

Largest lake Lake Victoria 68 800 sq km

Highest mountain Kilimanjaro 5892 m

Largest island Madagascar 587 040 sq km

N
W S E

EUROPE

Azores

Madeira

Canary Islands

Cape Verde Islands

Mediterranean Sea

Atlas Mountains

Sahara

Ahaggar 2918 ▲

Tibesti 3415

Qattara Depression

Libyan Desert

Sinai

R. Nile

Red Sea

Lake Nasser

ASIA

Gulf of Aden

R. Sénégal

R. Niger

R. Niger

R. Benue

Lake Chad

Lake Volta

Bioco

Gulf of Guinea

São Tomé

ATLANTIC OCEAN

Ascension Island

St Helena

R. White Nile

R. Blue Nile

Ras Dejen 4533 ▲

Lake Tana

Ethiopian Highlands

Lake Assal

Webi Shabeelle

Lake Turkana

INDIAN OCEAN

R. Ubangi

R. Congo

Congo Basin

R. Congo

Margherita Peak ▲ 5110

Great Rift Valley

Mount Kenya ▲ 5199

Lake Victoria

Kilimanjaro ▲ 5892

Lake Tanganyika

Bie Plateau

Lake Nyasa

R. Zambezi

R. Zambezi

Okavango Delta

Victoria Falls

Namib Desert

Kalahari Desert

R. Limpopo

R. Orange

R. Vaal

Drakensberg

Cape of Good Hope

Aldabra Islands

Comoro Islands

Mayotte

Mozambique Channel

Madagascar

Mauritius

Réunion

A Bedouin nomad in the Sahara Desert with his camels.

Kilimanjaro, an extinct volcano, is the highest mountain in Africa.

Scale : One centimetre on this map is the same as 450 kilometres on the ground.

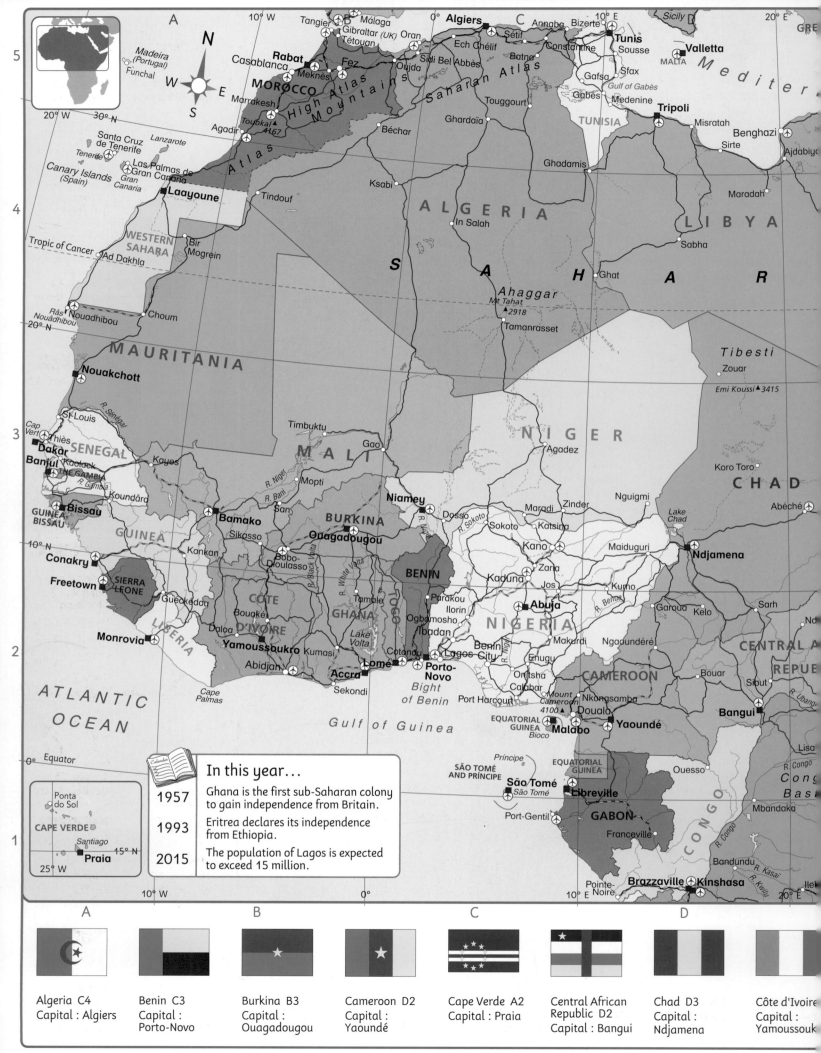

In this year...

1957	Ghana is the first sub-Saharan colony to gain independence from Britain.
1993	Eritrea declares its independence from Ethiopia.
2015	The population of Lagos is expected to exceed 15 million.

Algeria C4
Capital : Algiers

Benin C3
Capital : Porto-Novo

Burkina B3
Capital : Ouagadougou

Cameroon D2
Capital : Yaoundé

Cape Verde A2
Capital : Praia

Central African Republic D2
Capital : Bangui

Chad D3
Capital : Ndjamena

Côte d'Ivoire
Capital : Yamoussouk

Scale : One centimetre on this map is the same as 200 kilometres on the ground.

0   200   400   600   800 km

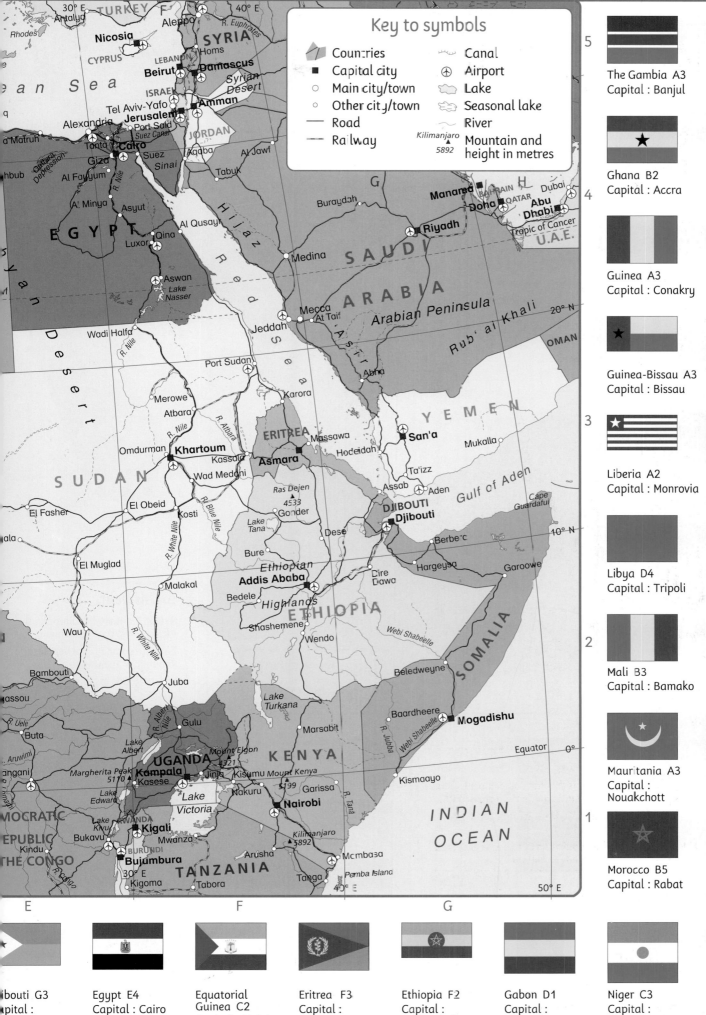

Key to symbols

Countries
Capital city
Main city/town
Other city/town
Road
Railway

Canal
Airport
Lake
Seasonal lake
River
Kilimanjaro 5892 ▲ Mountain and height in metres

The Gambia A3
Capital : Banjul

Nigeria C2
Capital : Abuja

Ghana B2
Capital : Accra

São Tomé and Príncipe C2
Capital : São Tomé

Guinea A3
Capital : Conakry

Senegal A3
Capital : Dakar

Guinea-Bissau A3
Capital : Bissau

Sierra Leone A2
Capital : Freetown

Liberia A2
Capital : Monrovia

Somalia G2
Capital : Mogadishu

Libya D4
Capital : Tripoli

Sudan E3
Capital : Khartoum

Mali B3
Capital : Bamako

Togo C2
Capital : Lomé

Mauritania A3
Capital : Nouakchott

Tunisia C5
Capital : Tunis

Morocco B5
Capital : Rabat

Uganda F2
Capital : Kampala

Djibouti G3
Capital : Djibouti

Egypt E4
Capital : Cairo

Equatorial Guinea C2
Capital : Malabo

Eritrea F3
Capital : Asmara

Ethiopia F2
Capital : Addis Ababa

Gabon D1
Capital : Libreville

Niger C3
Capital : Niamey

Western Sahara A4
Capital : Laayoune

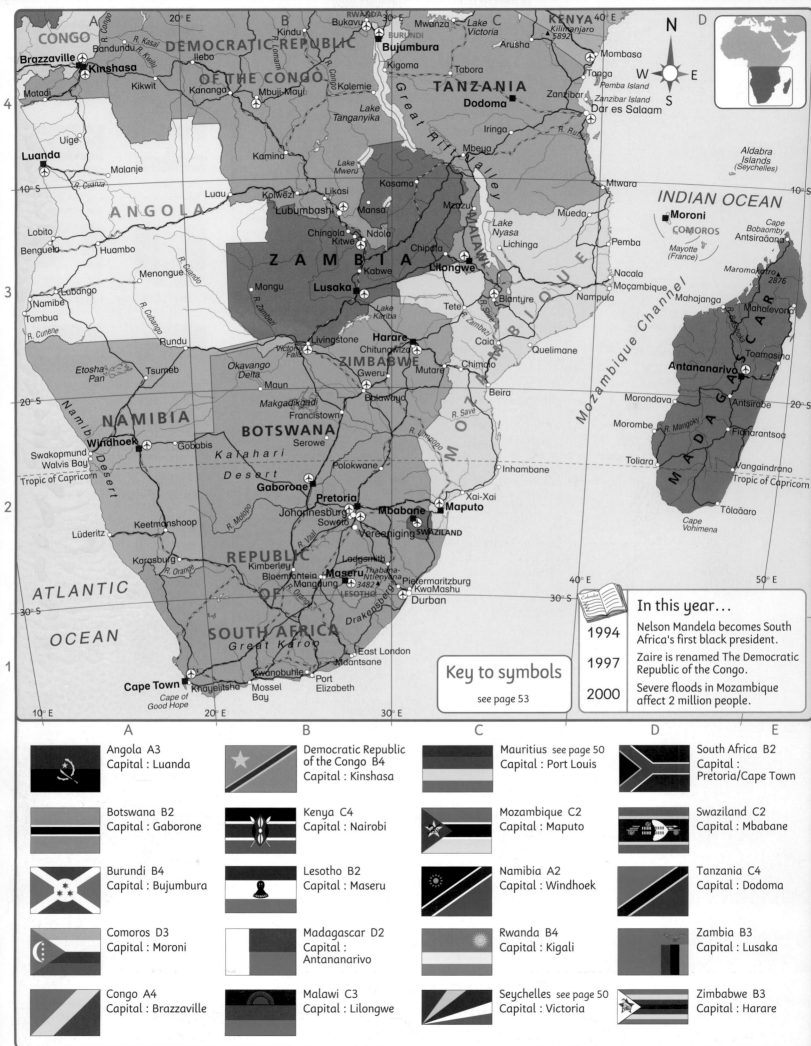

Key to symbols

see page 53

In this year...

1994 Nelson Mandela becomes South Africa's first black president.

1997 Zaire is renamed The Democratic Republic of the Congo.

2000 Severe floods in Mozambique affect 2 million people.

Angola A3
Capital : Luanda

Democratic Republic of the Congo B4
Capital : Kinshasa

Mauritius see page 50
Capital : Port Louis

South Africa B2
Capital :
Pretoria/Cape Town

Botswana B2
Capital : Gaborone

Kenya C4
Capital : Nairobi

Mozambique C2
Capital : Maputo

Swaziland C2
Capital : Mbabane

Burundi B4
Capital : Bujumbura

Lesotho B2
Capital : Maseru

Namibia A2
Capital : Windhoek

Tanzania C4
Capital : Dodoma

Comoros D3
Capital : Moroni

Madagascar D2
Capital :
Antananarivo

Rwanda B4
Capital : Kigali

Zambia B3
Capital : Lusaka

Congo A4
Capital : Brazzaville

Malawi C3
Capital : Lilongwe

Seychelles see page 50
Capital : Victoria

Zimbabwe B3
Capital : Harare

0   200   400   600   800 km

Scale : One centimetre on this map is the same as 200 kilometres on the ground.

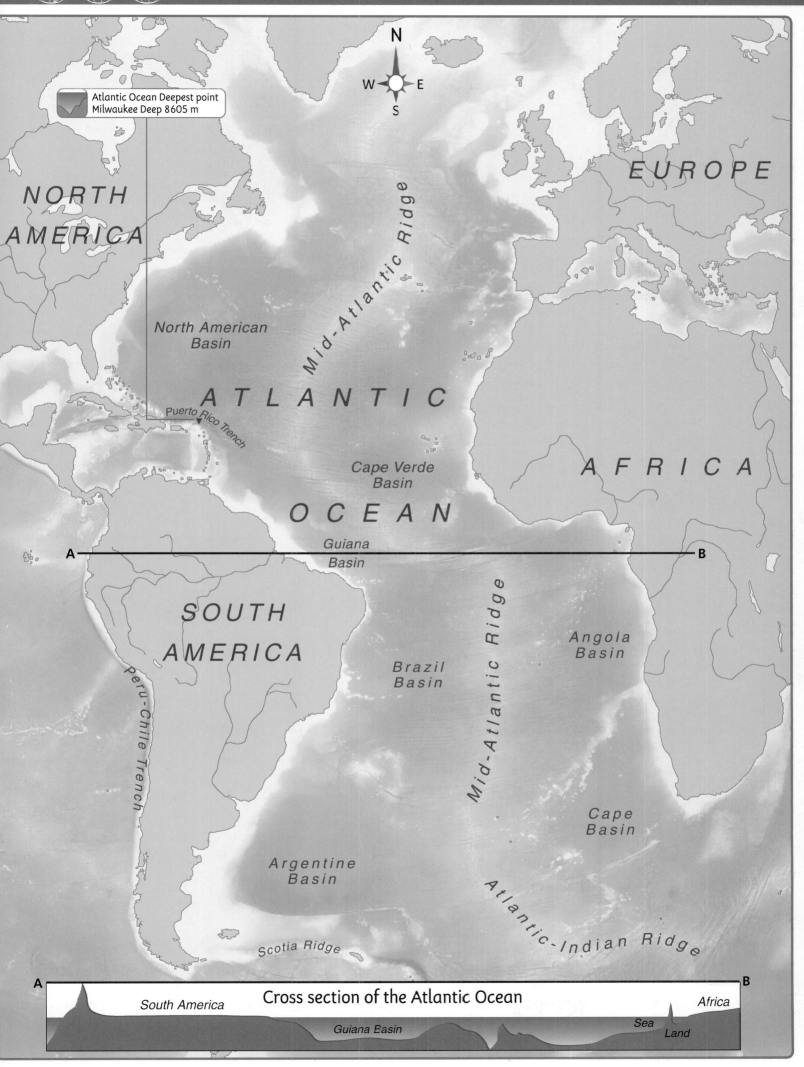

Atlantic Ocean Deepest point
Milwaukee Deep 8605 m

NORTH
AMERICA

EUROPE

North American
Basin

Mid-Atlantic Ridge

A T L A N T I C

Puerto Rico Trench

AFRICA

Cape Verde
Basin

O C E A N

A ———————— Guiana ———————— B
Basin

SOUTH
AMERICA

Brazil
Basin

Mid-Atlantic Ridge

Angola
Basin

Peru-Chile Trench

Cape
Basin

Argentine
Basin

Atlantic-Indian Ridge

Scotia Ridge

Cross section of the Atlantic Ocean

A

South America

B

Africa

Guiana Basin

Sea

Land

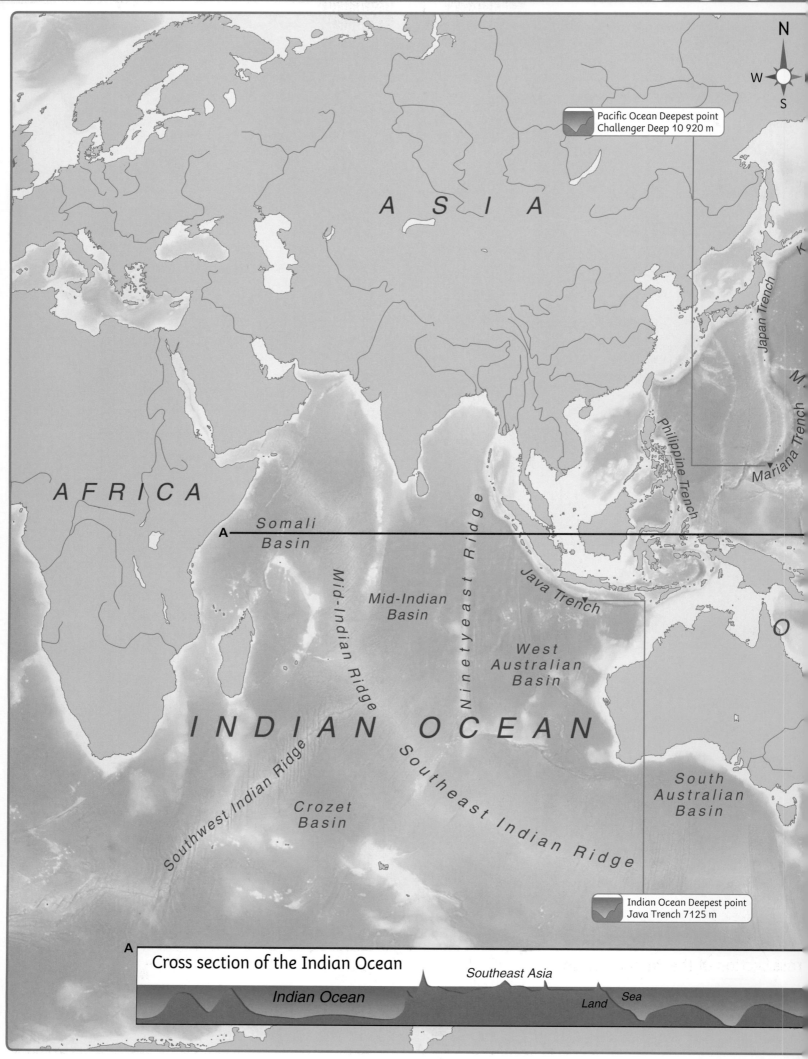

N
W · E
S

Pacific Ocean Deepest point
Challenger Deep 10 920 m

ASIA

AFRICA

Japan Trench

Mariana Trench

Philippine Trench

A — Somali
Basin

Mid-Indian
Basin

Ninetyeast Ridge

Java Trench

West
Australian
Basin

O

Mid-Indian Ridge

INDIAN OCEAN

Southwest Indian Ridge

Southeast Indian Ridge

South
Australian
Basin

Crozet
Basin

Indian Ocean Deepest point
Java Trench 7125 m

A

Cross section of the Indian Ocean

Southeast Asia

Indian Ocean

Land   Sea

Aleutian Trench

NORTH
AMERICA

thwest
acific
asin

Northeast
Pacific
Basin

Hawaiian Ridge

cific Mountains

Middle America Trench

Central
Pacific
Basin

P A C I F I C

East Pacific Rise

B

O C E A N

SOUTH
AMERICA

A N I A

Peru
Basin

Norfolk Island Ridge

Kermadec Trench   Tonga Trench

Peru-Chile Trench

Southwest
Pacific
Basin

Pacific-Antarctic Ridge

Southeast
Pacific
Basin

B

ross section of the Pacific Ocean

South America

Pacific Ocean

Key to symbols

Land height above sea level in metres

over 2000 ....
1000 – 2000 ....
500 – 1000 ....
200 – 500 ....
0 – 200 ....

- River
- Lake
- Ice cap
- Polar pack ice
- Drifting ice

In this year…

1969   The first surface crossing of the Arctic Ocean is completed.

2007   Area of Arctic ice falls to record low of 5.2 million sq km.

2007   A Russian expedition makes the first ever manned descent to the bottom of the ocean at the North Pole.

The British Isles at the same scale.

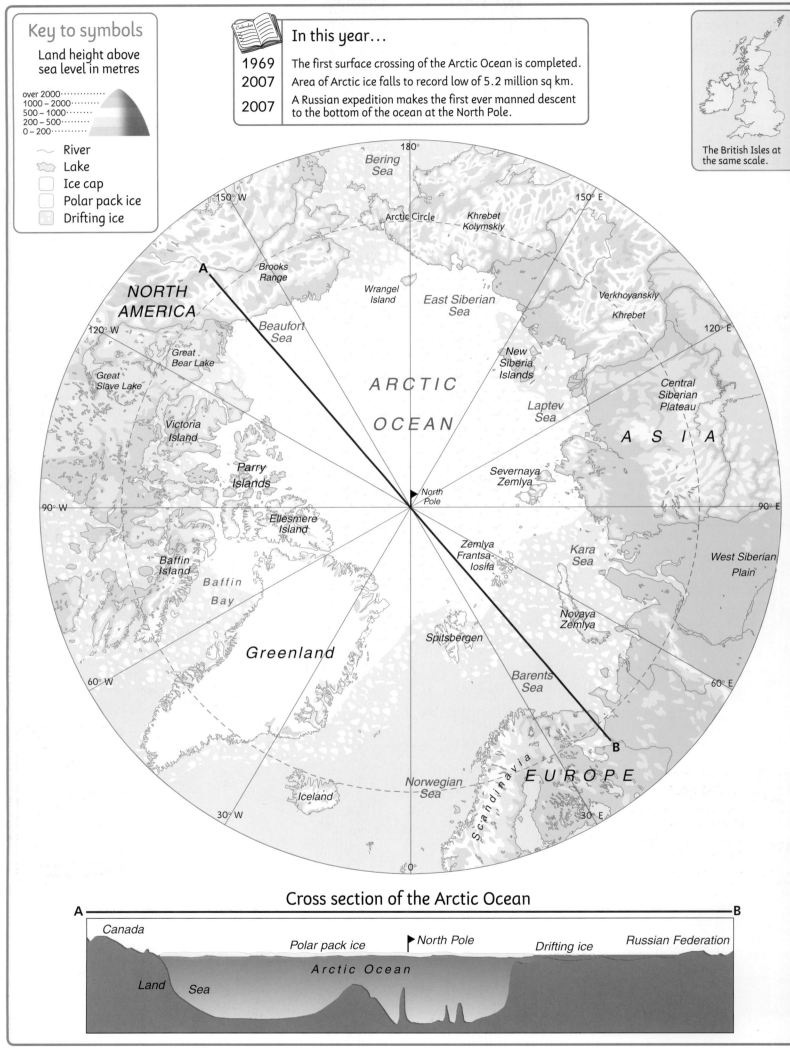

180°

Bering Sea

150° W

150° E

Arctic Circle

Khrebet Kolymskiy

Brooks Range

NORTH AMERICA

Wrangel Island

East Siberian Sea

Verkhoyanskiy Khrebet

120° W

120° E

Beaufort Sea

Great Bear Lake

New Siberia Islands

Central Siberian Plateau

ARCTIC

OCEAN

Laptev Sea

A S I A

Great Slave Lake

Victoria Island

Parry Islands

Severnaya Zemlya

90° W

North Pole

90° E

Ellesmere Island

Zemlya Frantsa-Iosifa

Kara Sea

West Siberian Plain

Baffin Island

Baffin Bay

Novaya Zemlya

Greenland

Spitsbergen

Barents Sea

60° W

60° E

Scandinavia

E U R O P E

Norwegian Sea

Iceland

30° W

30° E

0°

Cross section of the Arctic Ocean

A ———————————————————————— B

Canada

Polar pack ice

North Pole

Drifting ice

Russian Federation

Arctic Ocean

Land

Sea

0   500   1000   1500   2000 km

Scale : One centimetre on this map is the same as 350 kilometres on the ground.

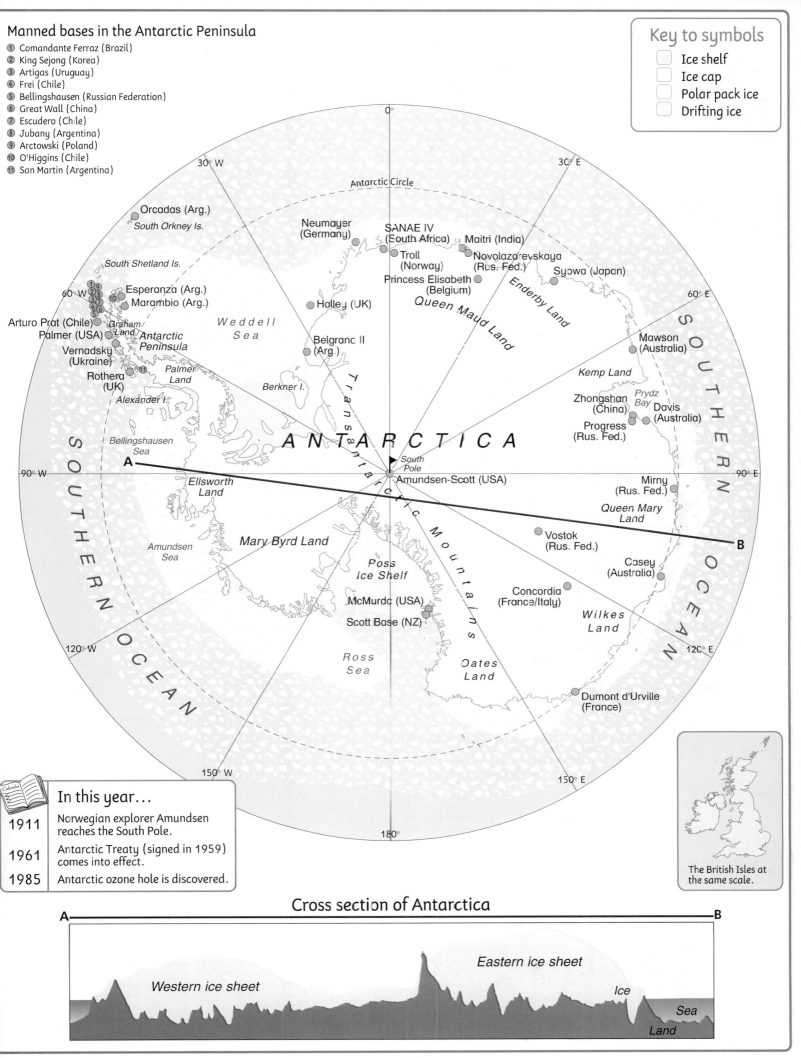

Manned bases in the Antarctic Peninsula

① Comandante Ferraz (Brazil)
② King Sejong (Korea)
③ Artigas (Uruguay)
④ Frei (Chile)
⑤ Bellingshausen (Russian Federation)
⑥ Great Wall (China)
⑦ Escudero (Chile)
⑧ Jubany (Argentina)
⑨ Arctowski (Poland)
⑩ O'Higgins (Chile)
⑪ San Martin (Argentina)

Key to symbols

- ☐ Ice shelf
- ☐ Ice cap
- ☐ Polar pack ice
- ☐ Drifting ice

In this year...

1911	Norwegian explorer Amundsen reaches the South Pole.
1961	Antarctic Treaty (signed in 1959) comes into effect.
1985	Antarctic ozone hole is discovered.

The British Isles at the same scale.

Cross section of Antarctica

Western ice sheet

Eastern ice sheet

Ice

Sea

Land

Scale : One centimetre on this map is the same as 350 kilometres on the ground.

500   1000   1500   2000 km

place name	grid code	place name	grid code	place name	grid code	place name	grid code
Cairo *capital* 53 F5		Tyne *river* 18 D4		Italy *country* 24 G3		Corsica *island* 24 F3	
page number		page number		page number		page number	
cities and towns are shown in green		water features are shown in blue		countries and states are shown in red		physical features are shown in black	

Photo credits

Science Photo Library:
p15 London, p16 UK Satellite image, p17 Beachy Head

Mark Steward:
p17 Glen Coe, p26 Kuala Lumpur, p35 Grand Canyon, p46 Sydney

Corbis:
p34 Times Square, Jose Fuste Raga, p42 Rio de Janeiro, Richard T. Nowitz

Still Pictures:
p13 Etna eruption, Otto Hahn, p14 Brussels, Wim Van Cappellen, p26 Shanghai, Markus Dlouhy, p43 Argentina, Galen Rowell, p43 Rainforest, Jacques Jangoux, p46 Solomon islander, K. Hympendahl, p47 Great Barrier Reef, Fred Bavendam, p47 Uluṟu, Raimund Franken, p50 Masai warriors, Friedrich Stark, p51 Sahara Desert, Frans Lemmens

Shutterstock:
p12 Colosseum, SF photo, p12 Eiffel Tower, Igor Rivilis, p13 Norway, Plotnikoff, p27 Rice paddies, Bali, Lim Yong Hian, p27 Mount Everest, Pichugin Dmitry, p34 Washington, Jonathan Larsen, p35 Niagara Falls, Howard Sandler, p42 Machu Picchu, Amy Nicole Harris, p47 Aoraki (Mount Cook), Sander van Sinttruye, p50 Cape Town, W. Woyke, p50 Giza, sculpies, p51 Kilimanjaro, enote

Acknowledgement

Editorial Adviser: Professor Simon Catling, pp2-7

Maps on the pages listed below are derived in part from material originally published in Collins Longman Atlases:
Keystart Junior Atlas: Pp8-9, p12, pp22-23, pp24-25, p26, p34, p42, p46, p50. Foundation Atlas: Pp58, p59